D...
THAT LIFE NEVER ENDS?

What if you *knew* positively, not just as a matter of belief, that you survived death? Right now, however strong your faith, you may *hope* there will be a hereafter, but you are not inwardly sure. This uncertainty in your own consciousness prevents you from looking ahead with any anticipation to the joining of those you love when your time comes to go.

How is it possible, then, for you to gain the inner spiritual assurance, the definite *knowing* feeling, the absolute faith that life does not end at the grave?

May I take you with me on the path I have trod through the wilderness of human thinking, the jungle of false concepts, the tangle of conflicting beliefs, the morass of prejudice and superstition, to final emergence into the clear, strong, revealing light of *inner knowledge* which is to be found, at last, within your own mind and soul?

Harold Sherman

Also by Harold Sherman:

YOUR KEY TO HAPPINESS

YOU
LIVE AFTER
DEATH

by HAROLD SHERMAN

With a new preface by the author   Revised edition

FAWCETT GOLD MEDAL • NEW YORK

ISBN 0-449-13798-8

Printed in Canada

First Fawcett Gold Medal Edition: November 1972
First Ballantine Books Edition: April 1984

To my mother

CONTENTS

YOU
LIVE AFTER
DEATH

PREFACE

SINCE THIS BOOK was written, often referred to as a classic of its kind, there has been increasing evidence in support of life after death.

Now, as founder and president of the ESP Research Associates Foundation, Little Rock, Arkansas, I receive hundreds of letters from men and women describing experiences they have had which they feel have proved the continued existence of their departed loved ones. These case histories tell of communication through dreams, visions, direct voice, apparitional visitations, contact through the Ouija board and automatic writing, psychic seances and messages through trance mediums, or as a result of out-of-body adventures. There are many different forms of psychic phenomena through which impressions may be received from purported discarnate intelligences—those who have left this earth life.

Every report must be carefully studied and weighed to make sure that the person professing to have had the experience has not been self-deluded or has not imagined the event or been the victim of hallucination or of a fraudulent medium.

There are, unhappily, so many psychic pitfalls for the inexperienced and the unwary—especially when an individual who has lost a loved one is so fervently desirous of finding some proof that he still lives. Such a person will often grasp at any happening or demonstration that, on the surface, would seem to indicate survival or an attempt to communicate.

The wide acceptance, even in some scientific circles, of mind-to-mind communication has made evident the possibility of mind-to-mind communication with those who have left this life, on the assumption that they continue to exist in a dimension as real to them as this life is to us. This also presumes that those who "die" retain not only their identity but their memory and their affection as well as their interest in loved ones and friends still on earth.

Those who believe in reincarnation feel that the soul must return to earth to atone for past mistakes and misdeeds in former lives before this soul can go on to higher planes of being.

There has always been controversy between believers and nonbelievers. There is, however, no conclusive evidence as yet that reincarnation is true. There are other possible explanations for seeming indications of reincarnation—such as possession by a discarnate spirit carrying over his memory of a past life on earth which the victim of possession mistakes as his own. Children brought up in homes where elders believe in reincarnation are highly suggestible and may imagine or fabricate past life experiences. A "possessing spirit" could so take over a child's body and mind that his own identity would be blanked out. This spirit could then locate his living relatives and friends, on occasion recalling past incidents and experiences which had taken place in his own past life, not the child's.

There is the possibility of genetic memory, wherein not only the physical but the mental characteristics of past ancestors are carried forward and the memory fragmentarily released in the mind of the descendant through a dream, vision, or feeling. Such an occasion, under hypnotic regression or other emotional conditions, could give a person the feeling that he had lived before, whereas this "remembered experience" could actually have happened to a previous decedent in the direct ancestral line.

Should any reader wish to test the validity of the reincarnation theory, all he has to do is to order "past life readings" offered for a fee in various metaphysical publications. Supposedly any medium who advertises the power to "tap the Akashic Records," where, we are told, a true report of all past lives is kept, can give you an accurate accounting of past lives as they affect the life you are now living.

I have sought such "knowledge" from a number of these past life readers and none of them have had any similarity—even in the same time cycle. According to them, I have been a woman and a man in the same period of time.

The readings have all stated emphatically, leaving no room for doubt, that these past life reports were true and should be accepted as such, and that I should regulate my present life in conformity in order to take full karmic advantage of the revelation. By so doing, I have been assured that I would thus lessen the number of lives I otherwise might have to experience on this earth, before I will have progressed sufficiently on this earth plane to win my release to "higher realms."

You can be sure, if proponents of reincarnation should be correct, that you will never see your loved ones again. He would be as dead to you as though he were nonexistent, since his sex as well as personality would be unrecognizably changed and all the interrelated experiences you have had with him would have no further value, with no possibility of renewal and continuance.

Believers in reincarnation tell us that we sometimes return as the mother or father of our earthly father or mother in this life, and a varied assortment of new relationships are suggested to help us learn certain lessons we failed to learn in past lives. This game of "musical chairs" is to continue *ad infinitum*. We inescapably develop new karma through new mistakes in each life which have to be expiated. We are on the endless wheel of incarnation and reincarnation, with relationships so mixed up that they have lost all identity as concerns us or our loved ones.

No believer in reincarnation has ever satisfactorily answered the question of where the souls of our loved ones are between incarnations—what they are doing while sitting around waiting for reentrance into this life. They are professedly absorbing the lessons of the immediate past life and choosing the kind of experience needed for further soul development. But where and under what conditions do our loved ones exist and who supervises their progression from one life to another?

Arthur Ford, world-famous medium, told me that in the thousands of communications he has received from the other side, there has not been one reference to a reincarnative experience. He has purportedly communicated with some discarnate entities who have left this life a hundred and more years ago. Contact could obviously not have been made had these entities reincarnated. Under such circumstances, the identities by which they had been known on earth would then have been forever lost to us.

In this brand-new edition of *You Live After Death,* I feel it necessary to emphasize these points because so many disturbed and confused men and women are writing me that they have been told their loved ones have been reincarnated or are due to be reincarnated, and that they should look for them to reveal their characteristics in newborn babies that have come or are destined to come to friends or relatives.

It is much more logical and inspiring to envision dimensions of existence beyond this life on earth where surviving entities continue their development, with the renewed opportunity to overcome there what they have failed to achieve here.

Overwhelming evidence is flowing in to our Foundation every day, as members, as well as readers of my books throughout the world, report their experiences, many well-witnessed and authenticated, pertaining to communication with those who have gone on. The "laboratory of human experience" will disclose (and has disclosed) more knowledge as well as more proof of continued existence beyond the physical, than all the scientific laboratories.

This is so because it is impossible to make those in the next life conform, with their different existing conditions, to the mechanical and physical limitations and restrictions placed upon them by academic investigators. As a consequence, many parapsychologists are commencing to go out in the field, away from their laboratories, to observe and analyze phenomena that are occurring spontaneously, and which can rarely, if ever, be reproduced or duplicated in the confines of the research facilities, however sensitized the instrumentation.

Stories are now appearing in newspapers and magazines, giving feature and headline attention to dramatic real-life cases suggestive of "spirit communication." One story which appeared recently, is an extraordinary example of "contact between worlds."

The locale of this happening was Portage, Indiana. A young man, Charles Troxell, 24, was murdered, his body punctured by bullets, stripped of identification, left by the roadside, his car stolen. Two days later his body was identified by his uncle, Donald Troxell of Gary. His father, Romer Troxell, 42, of Levittown, Pa., was notified and came to Portage, with his wife Edna, and daughter Romona. He did not know that the police were about ready to move in and arrest a youthful suspect. But as he stood, looking down at the face of his dead son, in the morgue, he was startled to hear the voice of his son speaking to him. "Hi, Pop. I knew you'd come. He's got my car."

Troxell said police were tight-lipped about their investigation and he and his family went to Gary to stay with his brother over the weekend.

"But I got restless on Monday," he said. "I started out in my car with my wife and sister-in-law, and began searching I don't know what for. *Charlie was going to guide me.*"

He drove along a road he did not know for about twenty minutes when, "I heard Charlie's voice saying, 'Here he comes, Pop.' "But," explained Troxell, "there was a hill ahead and no sign of any car.

"Then I saw the yellow Corvette coming over the crest and Charlie told me, "Here he comes, Pop. Take it easy. He's armed. Don't get excited. He's going to park soon."

"I made a U-turn and followed the car, about a block behind," Troxell said. "I wanted to crash into that yellow car but Charlie warned me against it."

Troxell followed the car and when it parked outside a high school, he went up to the youthful driver, later identified as Arthur Wagner, 18, who has been charged with the murder.

"The boy knew who I was," Troxell said. "He said he had seen my car at my brother's home."

Troxell asked the youth what he was doing with the car, and he said Charlie had sold it to him.

"Then he made a mistake," Troxell said. "The boy said he hadn't seen Charlie for two days and when I asked him if he was sure, he said, 'No, but isn't he dead?'

"I knew I had the killer because Charlie's identity had not been published in the paper yet; only the police and the family knew it," Troxell said.

"Then I asked the kid if he had bought the car, where was the title, and I heard Charlie's voice again. It said: 'Be careful, Pop. He's got a gun.' So I told the kid to forget the title (which was later found in the glove compartment of the car along with a .32 caliber pistol, with four spent shells, which police said was the murder weapon)."

While Troxell talked with the youth, police were enroute, summoned by the sister-in-law, who had slipped away.

"Charlie left me after we caught the killer." Troxell said. *"Charlie's in peace now*.

"The police were on to the killer, though," Troxell said. "I came to realize it when they later showed me what they uncovered in their investigation. *But when I heard my son guiding me, I acted. Maybe the Lord wanted it that way."*

Significance of This Psychic Experience

It would appear that the ordinary barrier between this world and the next is being broken down more and more as our minds become more receptive to the possibility of such communication.

It is necessary that some living mortal possess sufficient sensitivity for communication to take place. In this case, the father of the young man was the only one who heard his voice but it came through with such clarity and decisiveness that he could not mistake the directions given.

The awareness of the deceased son as to what was happening on earth and his ability to guide his father to the exact area where his killer was traveling is nothing short of astounding.

Of greater significance is the fact, as reported by the father, *"Charlie left me after we caught the killer."*

He "left" and "went somewhere," and the father had the impression that he was "now in peace."

There is no record that the son has returned since. This does not mean that he could not come back, having demonstrated that he could communicate this one time, but he undoubtedly saw no further need for staying around and was interested in giving his attention to the new life he had entered.

Those who have gone on have one great advantage over us. They *know* that they have survived death and that, in due course of time, we are destined to join them, so they can adjust to a temporary separation easier than we.

What Is "The Next Life" Like?

This question is often asked, and we have to depend upon the sketchy testimony of men and women who have had astral as well as cosmic experiences, either while near death, or during an out-of-the-body experience which has occurred involuntarily or under developed will control.

David Williams of Altoona, Pennsylvania has been able, since he was a young man to project himself into higher states of being. It was so seemingly natural to him that he thought, for quite a time, that everyone had this ability to a greater or lesser degree.

"My celestial experiences are fabulous," he reported recently, "in sights, colors, sounds, and sensations. The expanses are breathtaking and the colors are very intense and alive with feeling. I call it 'optic colors.' The stellar constellations are incredibly vivid, with a constant swirling state of activity. I have been drawn irresistibly to a certain group of stars, in the company of a guide, and taken to them at a tremendous rate of speed. But before I can travel, I have to step into a big ball of light, or fire, or whatever—molten gold in color.

"I have been to vast cities with very unusual looking buildings, impossible to describe. The colors are always much more intense than on earth. Sometimes I seem to be engaged as student, usually I just seem to be visiting.

"I have tested myself while in my astral body. A few months ago, I went straight through a glass window with both the window and me remaining intact. I went out through my bedroom window. It was peculiar to stand there, out of my physical body, and look up at the sky.

"I have heard transcendent music numerous times. One of the richest was an enormous choir of soldiers. You both hear and feel the music; it is a very *living* experience. Two times, I've heard a fantastic calliope."

Music From the World's Great Composers

We can no longer dismiss these extraordinary accounts as products of one's imagination and hallucinations. They are happening too often and too independently, one from the other, possessing a significant similarity.

While I have not, as yet, reported such experiences in my books, I, too, have heard exquisite music, sung by vast choirs or groups of singers, in what appeared to be vast stadiums, capable of holding as many as a million or more people.

And now an English medium and musician, Rosemary Brown, is winning world acclaim as the purported channel through which such world-famous composers as Liszt, Chopin, Beethoven, Debussy, Schubert, Schumann, Grieg, Brahms, and others are dictating from the spirit world new compositions which music critics say are remarkably reminiscent of these composers' styles.

Sir George Trevelyan, one of the many prominent people in London who have investigated Rosemary Brown's work, had this to say about her in the Psychic News, an internationally known spiritualistic weekly newspaper, in London.

"The phenomenon presents a challenge and is so unusual that it cannot be quickly dismissed by some facile explanation.

"It all began," says Sir George, "when Rosemary, as a girl, heard 'heavenly music' in her head. One day, an elderly man, later identified as Liszt, appeared to her clairvoyantly and told her that, in due time, he and other great composers would 'give her beautiful music and teach her how to play it.'

"Rosemary had no special musical talent. She had a few piano lessons before the war and could play the piano tolerably well. During the war, she contracted polio, but recovered sufficiently to begin to play again.

"She is a widow, of little means, confronted with the task of bringing up two children. Apparently, as a natural sensitive, she was chosen by Liszt and his fellow composers because she had no special talent and training, and could thus be taught from the other side of life much easier than had she been an accomplished musician with already established patterns and techniques of playing.

"In my observation, each composer works with her in his individual way. She is aware of them as if someone had simply walked into the room. She remains totally conscious and talks with her 'spirit teachers' as friends.

"The listener, of course, (someone like myself when present) hears only one side of the conversation.

"I was present on one occasion when she was receiving music from Chopin. There was nothing eerie or spooky about it. Chopin gave her a piece which she worked out phrase by phrase directly on the piano and in twenty minutes had it memorized and completed.

"Musicians will have some conception of what this feat means. There were moments when she even argued with Chopin about notes or rendering.

"Then Bach came. His approach was very different. She

had to reach for score paper and set down complete phrases dictated note by note.

"He was followed by Beethoven, whom Rosemary described as completely recognizable. His method was to impress music 'directly into her thinking in a manner which transcends our time sense, so that she heard a symphony within ten minutes.'

"Liszt, on the other hand, 'allows her always to play the whole piece' and then often helps her by using her hands in difficult passages.

"The result is that Rosemary, starting with a very limited piano technique, is able to master works far beyond that of the normal music student, even one who starts with much greater talent."

This testimony by Sir George Trevelyan has endorsement of trained musicians, composers, and scientists—all of whom declare that something most unusual is taking place, whether or not they accept as true that Rosemary Brown is actually receiving spirit-dictated compositions direct from this deceased assemblage of the world's greatest in the realm of music.

Sir George speculates that: "In the present critical human situation, it might well be that the 'higher worlds' intended to use music as a redemptive and healing force. Above all, perhaps it is intended to demonstrate survival beyond death so that this great source of doubt and fear in our materialistic age could be dispelled."

Communication in the "Here" and "Hereafter"

I wish it were possible to open up the voluminous files of our ESP Foundation and let you scan the hundreds and hundreds of case histories received from men and women in all walks of life, each describing often dramatic and always heart-touching "psychic experiences" they have had, presenting convincing evidence that "life does not end at the grave," that, instead, as the Bible so beautifully states, "Eye has not seen, nor ear heard the wonders that God holdeth in store for them who love Him."

I have selected one case from the many, to report here, because it is so representative, and because I have met and talked to Mrs. Frances Averill Messner, of Cadillac, Michigan, and can vouch for her utter sincerity and truthfulness as well as the possession of rare spiritual gifts.

Mrs. Messner is today a widow, aged 69, doing voluntary work for the organization FISH, caring for the emergency needs of people, and teaching illiterates without charge, how to read and write by the Laubach method. She graduated from the University of Michigan in 1922, taught high-school English, and for thirteen years served as head of the Congregational Church School. After her husband died, she went as a missionary to Athens, Greece, and taught in Pierce College for the American Church.

This background will help you appreciate her dedication to a life of service. This attitude of selflessness may have contributed to the development of the unusual sensitivity Mrs. Messner has possessed since a child.

Let her tell you some of her early experiences in ESP, as a prelude to her later life adventures in the realm of spirit.

"As a young girl, I always knew when trains were coming long before anyone else could hear them even by listening intently. Soon after Charles and I were married, I was teaching a class, suddenly threw my hand up to my head, put the class to work, and went down to the office, where I phoned my husband's office and told them there that the men on their way to Detroit had had an accident. I asked them to stand by to hear in about half an hour, to find out details and to call me. They thought I was just a nervous young bride, but it was true. The car had turned over and Charles had come down on his head.

"If urgent calls came in when Charles was not at home, I could project 'feelers' out and 'locate' him accurately, so that the business could be completed by the callers making another call to places otherwise unknown to me.

"Once I was doing the washing on a Saturday. I dropped everything and got to my parents' home about twenty-four miles away, just in time to fight a grass fire which had been started by a passing train. They would not

have been able to save their home without my opportune
and strenuous help.

"While I was in Athens, after my mother and husband
had left this life, I spent some time with my mother, and
later with Charles, where they were. They did not come to
me. I went to them. But I was not conscious of how I got
there or returned. In each case, I wrote out what had
taken place, and am responding to your request for personal testimony of this kind, for the inspiration and assurance it may give to others who have lost loved ones."

My "Heavenly Visit" with Mother

"During the night of July 10, 1958, I was with my mother.
I was floating through the air at her side, without effort
on our parts. It was a most pleasant experience; I could
realize her love for me as a real, accepted fact, and I, in
turn, felt very loving toward her. Our love was all-pervasive
without any self-consciousness. She was wearing a lovely
Botticelli angel shift of soft, delicate transparent stuff, rip-
pling as we flew without exercise or effort.

"Age as years (she died at 83) was not apparent, only
an effulgence of health and beauty. Her transparent body
had nothing on but this thin shift, and I was happy to no-
tice that her feet and hands were perfect, once very mis-
shapen with arthritis. Our hands were holding lightly with
arms at our sides. She was taking me to see many things in
many places; but I do not remember any of them except
the lovely flowers in the high natural grass we flew over.
I was happier than being with my mother ever had made
me. There was nothing but peace and love and joy sur-
rounding us."

My "Measureless Time" Spent with My Husband

"In one night, February 22, 1959, I spent a great long
time unmeasured by hours, days, nights, weeks, or years
with Charles, where he lives now. Never have I been in
such clear, fresh air; it was perfect! The light, too, was beyond any experience of mine. There was no glare or ex-

cessive brightness. We were in a magnificent habitation beyond Frank Lloyd Wright's earthly possibilities. The walls were not fixed but came and went with our thoughts. They were nebulous, evanescent, with much color! Possibly the walls were there because I am still in the material expression of life—to make me more at home. I am sure it was his heavenly home. It was full of softly luminous awareness, rather than lighting.

"So different from his life on earth, Charles had no interest or desire or wish or thought in relation to TV or any form of earthly pleasures or pastimes. When I was with Mother, I was delighted with the perfection of her hands and feet, and noticed her body and what she was wearing. Also, she had her eyes closed, and I was at her side with feelings communicating between us.

"With Charles, I was directly before him and never noticed anything about him except his eyes, radiant with love, pouring right into my eyes. He seemed to be made of golden light. Even now when I think of being there with him, I know what heaven is; I have seen faith itself. He had no shadow of doubt about anything anywhere. Perfect calm joy!

"Eternity will never be too long to commune. Anyone would be glad to go there. I will never dread dying. At the same time I realize that I must continue to do my part in the materially expressing world. Of one thing I feel sure: it does not matter into what stage of development we graduate from the earth school, God loves us completely and progress is sure for all."

These glimpses of the "afterlife," as reliably reported now by so many, are just different enough as well as possessing an underlying similarity to indicate the variety of spiritual adventures awaiting each and everyone of us when our turn comes to experience the change called death.

In the years since *You Live After Death* was written I have seen no reason to alter any of it. Everything I wrote is even truer today.

It is my hope that a careful reading and study of this little volume will forever remove your fear of death, and provide you with an inner comfort and assurance to greatly relieve your grief if you have been separated for a time, short at the longest, from the physical presence of a loved one.

May it also bring you in closer communion with whatever your concept may be of God, the Great Intelligence, to whom you owe your creation, and whose "many mansions of existence" await your arrival, as you continue the evolution of your soul beyond the boundaries of this planet Earth, which has given to you your first life experience.

Again, I am indebted to Frances Averill Messner, for this inspired spiritual statement which she feels was "given" to her, and which she has granted me permission to give to you. In the years that I have studied and sought to develop and demonstrate these higher powers of mind, I have been led more and more to seek and to express the spiritual side of extrasensory perception. When one does this, one is brought more and more into an awareness of the God Presence, which Mrs. Messner so beautifully stresses in the words you are about to read.

Apply them now to yourself, as you prepare your mind and heart to receive the message contained for you in *You Live After Death.*

Father God, I become still to know YOU,
the only good, the all-powerful good.
YOU dwell within me
In the "secret place of the Most High."
YOU have given me YOURSELF,
even as the ocean is in the wave,
but I have often foolishly felt and acted
    as if I were alone
without any strength but my own separate weakness.

I am not a dry, lifeless twig;
I am a living "branch"—fruitful
with my life from the "VINE."

Here, sheltered from the world,
I know the reality of YOUR Presence
within me and within every other person
every instant, continuously,
so that I may learn YOUR will,
so that, loving YOU in myself and in my neighbor,
    I will learn
to do YOUR work with YOU,
to do YOUR continuing creation in the world
as YOU DO
through me or any listening person
willing to do YOUR will.
                    Selah

1. IS THERE A PERSONAL GOD?

WHEN YOU DIE, will you survive death?

Will you continue to exist in some higher physical form, in a world seemingly as real and as rational as this? Will you meet and associate with those you love there? Will you retain a memory of your earth experiences and will you recognize those you hold dear on sight? Will you find yourself in heaven, a place of golden streets, with hosts of human souls playing on harps and singing praises to God, as pictured in religious versions of the hereafter? Or will you find yourself in an existence not too unlike your state on earth, with duties to perform, responsibilities to assume, and opportunities for development which may have been denied you here?

These questions, and many more, you may have asked others or yourself without obtaining any definite, satisfying, logical answers. Either that, or you have not dared let yourself think of these questions and have put off facing them as long as possible. But, inevitably, you will be brought face to face with the immemorial cry of untold millions of grief-stricken, faith-torn, wondering and doubting humans: "If a man die, shall he live again?"

It is strange but nonetheless true that the average man or woman, during a lifetime, has given little earnest thought to this most important of all questions. Death is an unpleasant subject to contemplate and one which most humans—probably yourself among them—seek to avoid thinking about until the passing of a close friend or relative, or a serious illness of their own, compels them to do so. Even then, the minister usually steps in and cushions your grief by quoting spiritual phrases, words of faith and hope, designed to dispel all thoughts of doubt and wonderment and to assure you that "the one you love is not dead but still lives in the kingdom not of this world."

Religion, however, in offering spiritual consolation and assurance, has always been vague in its statements concerning the specific nature of any after-life. Heaven is described as a place having no location except that we have been led to picture it as *above* and hell as *below*.

Since the very foundation of the Christian faith is a belief in resurrection and a hereafter, it would seem that this religion should speak more authoritatively and definitely about life after death. Instead, you are asked to accept the fact of survival entirely on faith. No proof whatsoever is offered you.

In the event you should desire to know more of this "bourne from which no traveler returns" and to use your own *reason* in an attempt to gain a more realistic concept of conditions after death, you are told that "you know all you are supposed to know . . . that you mustn't doubt . . . and that you must accept this promise of eternal life on *faith* alone."

Science, until recent times, has not been helpful or even encouraging. The possibility of "life after death" has been dismissed by most scientists, who have held that man's possession of an immortal soul is very much to be doubted and that man dies when his body dies.

Today, however, science has pushed back the frontiers of its knowledge to such an astounding degree that it actually is offering more concrete evidence of man's possible survival than the churches! At the present rate of progress, science seems destined to reveal and to verify the truth of man's inherent relationship to God, the Great Intelligence, which faith has discerned through *inspiration* but has not been able to prove.

In the not too distant future, the greatest of all human fears—fear of death—may be largely dispelled in the light of man's deeper understanding of his own self. At present, literally millions of humans are afraid to think for themselves—to ponder the question of what happens to them when they die. And yet, if each of us actually survives death in a *self-conscious* state and under conditions at least as happy as those on earth, there is no fact in our entire life even remotely comparable in possible value or significance!

What if you *knew* positively, not just as a matter of belief, that you survived death? Right now, however strong your faith, you may *hope* there will be a hereafter, but you are not inwardly sure. You may fervently desire that you will one day see those you love again, yet your faith needs constant restoration through Bible reading, philosophic study, ministerial reassurance, and wishful thinking. This uncertainty in your own consciousness prevents you from looking ahead with any anticipation to the joining of those you love when your time comes to go. For you, heaven is not the desirable place constantly being pictured by spiritual leaders, for otherwise you would contemplate with great eagerness the adventure of death and the transition to a higher state of being.

How is it possible, then, for you to gain this inner spiritual assurance, the definite *knowing* feeling, the absolute faith that life does not end at the grave and that there awaits you and those you love an opportunity, in new dimensions, for the further evolvement of your own souls?

You can do what I have found it necessary to do in my own search for the truths underlying all basic religious faiths—truths which concern the existence of eternal and infallible mental and spiritual, universal principles which remain unchanged by individual interpretations of past, present, and future.

May I take you with me on the path I have trod through the wilderness of human thinking, the jungle of false concepts, the tangle of conflicting beliefs, the morass of prejudice and superstition, the barriers of formalized religion, to final emergence into the clear, strong, revealing light of *inner knowledge* which is to be found, at last, within your own mind and soul . . .?

Perhaps I can save you long years on the journey, the heartache of disillusionment, the terror you might experience in the night of doubt, the fear of losing what little faith you have in the perplexing maze of diverse theories and beliefs, the shock of spiritual deception at the hands of charlatans, and the loss of confidence in, and respect for, the integrity of humans whom you have almost worshiped for their purported possession of spiritual powers.

These are the soul bruises you would encounter along the way, some of which you may already have suffered in your own quest for a more satisfying, logical answer to the timeless mystery of death. But in the short cut to the knowledge and comfort you seek, you can bypass time-consuming, emotionally disturbing experiences and come with me into the presence of your own inner self, where the truth resides and the evidence of things unseen exists.

No, the solution of this mystery is not contained in the philosophies and religions of the world, nor in the outward practices and ceremonies and professions of men. And this is why the question of life after death has so long remained, for most humans, unsolvable.

Life has been so designed by an Infinite Wisdom that it contains the answer to its own riddle within itself! You and every human, therefore—who sincerely desires to know, "When I die, shall I live again?" must find this answer *within* yourself as a *personal experience*.

This will require a development of your own mind and soul. Such a development will, in time, enable you to reach higher centers of your own being, to receive inspiration and knowledge from higher sources than human, and to gain the assurance that a world exists beyond this which is as real as the one you are now in—perhaps even more so!

The path to this self-development is not easy, nor is the attainment of anything which is exceedingly worth while in this life. Now that the one way has been revealed to you, are you willing to persevere in proving for yourself that:

(1) You are a part of God, the Great Intelligence, in process of eternal evolvement;

(2) that this life is but the beginning of an ever-continuing unfolding of your real inner self.

I promise you a most exciting and rewarding experience of lasting value if you will accompany me from this point on. But you will have to resolve to hold an open, receptive mind at all times if you would make contact with the true world of spirit which lies beyond your physical senses.

Such a resolve will call for the exercise of courage and freedom from the fear of what others may think. You have been told for so long that faith is the only real answer to things of the spirit that you may be going against prevailing opinion in setting out to develop yourself spiritually.

But, remember this: life is an individual proposition . . . and no one can live it for you or experience it for you or interpret it for you. You can attain to higher and finer things only through your own free will so to do!

Just as no one can live for you, it should now be equally obvious that no one can die for you. We must each face death for ourselves. This being true, it is nothing short of folly for us not to give more serious thought and reflection to the great change which we eventually must face. This change might come tomorrow or even later today in the uncertainties of present-day life.

Were you planning on a long trip to a new and unfamiliar country, would you not prepare for such a journey to the very best of your knowledge and ability? Would you not consider it advisable to learn, before departure, all you could about this land and its residents and customs and what you might encounter there? It would be to your material advantage to have this information so that you could develop or obtain such resources as you might be lacking in order to meet the new and different conditions in this unknown territory. No explorer starts on an expedition who has not anticipated and made preparation for every possible need and contingency.

When death occurs, granted that there is a life beyond, you will be precipitated into it without warning and with only the mental and spiritual equipment you have acquired and developed through life experience. You may then discover that many of the things you considered so essential on earth are not only excess baggage in this next state of being but, because of your desperate clinging to them, are actually liabilities. Therefore your entire sense of values as established here is apt to be exploded unless you have developed a set of values on earth which will stand the test of time and change and growth.

The basic question of survival is associated with the question of whether or not there is a personal God. Man can conceive of a life after death if there exists in the universe a personal God interested enough in his creation to have provided for the survival of man in some self-conscious form. Otherwise the forces of nature seem too impersonal in their manifestation to have made man an exception among all created things by granting him immortal life.

Feeling this need of personal relationship between himself and his unknown Creator, man has felt impelled to create a concept of God not too unlike himself in order that he might establish a kinship with this Being.

It should be understandable to you, as you use your reason, how this came about. It is difficult, intelligent as you may be, not to visualize God, the Father, as seated somewhere on a throne, existing in some majestically glorified human form, and administering love, mercy, and justice to all creation. If you are a follower of the Christian faith, you will picture the risen Christ seated on the right hand of God. Should you be a follower of the faith of Mohammed, Confucius, Buddha, or any other religious sect, you will have a different concept of God which you may consider the only true one.

Yet it should be clear to any thinking individual that all concepts cannot be right, and there is a strong likelihood, in the still crude state of our enlightenment, that no one of these concepts presents a complete and accurate picture of this Indescribable Intelligence to which we owe our existence.

Thus, that you may prepare your mind for attaining a

true and ever-increasing spiritual awareness of the universe as it *is,* you can see that it is primarily necessary for you to enlarge your concept of God. Have no fear that this releasing of the old and taking on of the new concept will destroy your faith, for the greater you can conceive a God of this universe to be, the more logical becomes the possibility that such a Creator has the power to provide for the "salvation" of all his worthy creatures.

All religions today are undergoing severe external and internal pressures due to the fact that they have sought to hold to old standards, old moralities, and old concepts in a rapidly changing world. We have evidence on every side that nothing on earth is standing still. Change is inherent in everything. This is a universal law. The cellular structure of your body and its chemistry is being altered as you read these words. The aging process is incessantly going on. Without change there could be no progress or development.

In a time when knowledge is being vastly increased in the sciences of physics, chemistry, biology, botany, astronomy, medicine, mathematics, and every other subject and type of activity in this world, religion alone is trying to maintain a stationary position. It is considered sacrilegious, even blasphemous, to challenge any of the ancient concepts of God and the creeds supporting these concepts. Orthodox religionists seem to feel that a surrender of views long held as the word of God would be an admission of loss of faith and a sin punishable by loss of salvation.

It is tragically unfortunate that man, in his early desire to establish a spiritual relationship between his concepts of God and himself, did not provide in the tenets of his different religions for an expansion of these concepts in keeping with the advancement of man's own intelligence. Life experience demands and has demanded, that man use his brain in meeting and solving all problems except those of religion, where he is exhorted to rely only upon his faith.

Because of the Church's demand for blind and unthinking allegiance to its spiritual doctrines, the rank and file of its members have placed dependence upon a spiritual power *outside* themselves and have not, as a consequence, been impressed with the necessity for developing the spiritual powers they themselves possess *within* their own minds and souls. Faith has been stressed as all that is fundamentally needed for salvation. The sinner may confess, have faith, be forgiven, and be saved.

Do you yourself feel—if you are a professed believer in some religion—that your faith and membership before God assures the salvation of your soul? Have you been inspired, as a result of your religious teachings, to devote thought and effort each day to the development of your spiritual nature, as a means of enriching your present life experience and building qualities of character which might quite logically lead to storing up treasures in heaven? Have you been given any technique for right thinking which, conscientiously employed by you, would lead to a better understanding of your own self, your fellow man, and your relation to God, the Great Intelligence? Or have you, for the most part, been talked to in spiritual generalities and presented an endless repetition of Biblical stories based on conditions existing in a small section of the world, in the life of one race of people, two thousand and more years ago?

Could a scientist of today depend upon the knowledge and wisdom of a people or a leader, however well endowed, of that age or time? Such a people or leader might well have discovered or rediscovered a spiritual principle and code of living so fundamental as to be of value to succeeding generations, but only as these generations, with their added experience and enlightenment, might apply this principle to the kind of world in which they then lived.

The mistake, then, that all religions have made has been in their worship of the *form* rather than the *spirit* of their doctrine. By worship of the form, they have kept it unchanged through the centuries and have imprisoned the spirit. For this very reason, religion has largely destroyed its spiritual effectiveness by denying to man his God-given right to expand spiritually as he is expanding in every other phase of his existence.

Man, today, has been kept in bondage, led to believe

that he can approach God only through certain established religious procedures. He is a lost soul in the eyes of the Church if he is not a member of some denomination, even though he may be one of a community's most respected citizens, an individual of unimpeachable character and spiritual attainment. This implies that God, Himself, is a being of narrow-minded, uncharitable, and sadistic stature who would condemn one of His own creation, however spiritually minded, for not having professed his faith as a member of some organized religion.

Reason tells you that the God of this universe is not such a God and that, therefore, man's concept of God must be narrow-minded, uncharitable, and sadistic if he would so legislate against his fellow man "outside the fold."

In all justice, either true spiritual development of any human creature, with or without church affiliation, brings automatically its own reward on earth, or in any state after death, or *all* spiritual development, as such, means nothing. Any just God, worthy of our love and worship, would not play favorites with individual members of His creation.

What happens to the old concept of God when you consider the possibility, as scientists and astronomers are now pointing out, that there may actually be untold millions of planets capable of sustaining life throughout the boundless reaches of time and space? If there are, then there must be many planets containing forms of life and intelligence similar to our own and, in numerous instances, vastly superior. These beings would be no less God's creatures than we are, for there can conceivably be only one Creator. It would certainly be presumptuous for us, knowing what we now know about the universe, to persist in the time-worn contention that God created the earth and placed the stars in the heavens just for us, and that we here on earth are the only intelligent beings having a right to survival throughout all time and space.

If intelligent life exists on other planets, then it is reasonable to suppose that this life has also developed its concept of God.

If the only way to God is through His only begotten Son, who visited this earth, what chance for salvation would souls of human status have on other worlds?

Would it have been necessary for God to have had His Son born and crucified upon each of the planets in order to have brought an opportunity for salvation to them?

What would have happened here if Christ had not been crucified? Would we have the Christian religion today? Would we even have preserved the record of a great and good man who lived and died nineteen hundred years ago? Do Christians now owe a profound debt, in fact the very existence of their religion, to those who crucified Christ?

With these questions in mind and attributing to God the power of knowing the end from the beginning, then are we to believe that He ordained the crucifixion of His Son? If God had the power to send His Son to earth, He had the power to have protected Him against this crucifixion.

But our whole Christian faith depends upon the belief that Christ died on the cross in atonement for our sins and, after three days, rose from the dead, giving us the promise of resurrection as a reward for our faith in Him. Millions of humans have endured as great if not greater torture and suffering unto death, so this in itself gives no distinction to the experience of Christ on Calvary. In India today, in our time, another great and good man has died a martyr to his spiritual convictions of passive resistance patterned after the life of Christ. Mohandas K. Gandhi will surely be as sainted in the minds and hearts of his followers for all time to come, and the memory of his beneficent presence among them, his sufferings, privation, and sacrifices on their behalf, will be just as revered as our memory of the Man of Galilee.

How, then, shall we view the great spiritual leaders of all time, including Christ? Might it not be possible that there are spiritually illumined sons and daughters of God's creation on all planets where creatures on the level of human intelligence, or higher, exist? Such spiritual leaders could be truly termed sons of God by virtue of their self-attained mental and spiritual powers—powers not bestowed through some miracle of birth but developed by these individuals through life experience, revealing to them a knowledge of the laws of God transcending that of their fellow creatures in whatever age and state of advancement they may have lived.

God, in the universality of His presence, could not and would not reveal Himself in any one moment of time to a small and segregated portion of His creation. But, in and through nature, God, the Great Intelligence, reveals Himself continually to all creatures, in all places and at all times, at whatever level of understanding these creatures have achieved. Thus their concepts of God are constantly expanding in keeping with their advancing enlightenment.

The revelation of God is written forever in nature and not in the words of man. To find God and to know Him is, then, to search Him out in the soul of all things, to feel His presence in everything you think and do, and to gain the awareness through right thinking and meditation that a part of God, the Great Intelligence, actually dwells within your own consciousness.

When this realization comes to you, as it can and will if you earnestly strive to develop your inner powers of spiritual perception, you will then know for a certainty that because you are a self-conscious part of God in evolutionary unfolding, your body form may change but you, yourself, your soul, your identity, that something which says, "I am I" to you, cannot and does not die. You will have found, beyond creed, beyond doubt, beyond all narrow and confining religious concepts, that personal contact with God, the Father, you have long sought. And your faith in His power and goodness will be supported by the evidence of your own inner life experience.

This, then, is the foundation for your entrance upon the great adventure of personally finding and knowing God. You are ready to give thought to the nature of your own soul and what you may do to develop it while on Earth in preparation for the life to come!

2. DO YOU POSSESS A SOUL?

THE BELIEF that man possesses a soul dates back to thousands of years before Christ.

The earliest races of humans held varying concepts that something in man survived his body and continued to live in some vague and often shadowy or nebulous state after death. They feared the dark as a symbol of the unknown world about them, welcomed the day and dreaded the night.

In those ancient times, before men knew the earth was round, every natural catastrophe such as a flood, an earthquake, a cyclone, a great fire, a pestilence, a flaming comet, or any force or occurrence visiting disaster upon them was interpreted as the work of demons—mysterious, invisible beings who dwelt in darkness or the bowels of the earth. The sun, giver of light, was worshiped as a supreme god, and there were many lesser gods of nature to whom these primitive peoples gave their homage in appreciation of beneficent acts.

There was, then, the recognition that forces greater than man were working in and through and about him, having an influence upon his life, either for good or evil. In man's ignorance and fear, he felt there was no escaping these influences and, believing himself helpless in their presence, he endeavored to placate them by offering up prayers and sacrifices of his choicest possessions. Sometimes the finest young men of the race and the most beautiful virtuous maidens were burned or hurled to their death in an attempt to appease the imagined wrath of the gods or demons responsible for some cataclysmic happening or plague.

Thus we have the origin in antiquity of man's blood sacrifice in striving to atone for misdeeds or win the favor of special gods. Carried on down to more recent centuries, we have the outstanding example of blood sacrifice with God being represented as offering up His Son on the cross.

In all recorded and unrecorded history we have little evidence that mankind has ever sought to correct and eliminate its sins of the flesh by making a concerted effort toward the self-development of higher and finer spiritual powers. Instead, humans of all ages, in all races, have been willing to sacrifice the innocent and to let someone else do the suffering for the evils they have committed.

For this reason, while man has persisted in his belief that he possesses a soul, he has done almost nothing to develop this soul within him. He has, however, aligned himself with different religious sects as a means of insuring his salvation on the basis of faith alone. This, he has been told, is all that is required of him in this life as a guarantee of his participation in the life to come.

But ask man to define his soul, to tell you what he thinks it consists of, what its substance may be, and of what qualities and faculties it is comprised, and he has only the vaguest of concepts. He may confess he's never thought much about it since he has not expected to meet up with it or have use for it until death occurs. He has been perfectly willing to let his pastor worry about his soul and pray for it while he goes about the ordinary business of living. His soul then, whatever it is, is left pretty much to take care of itself.

The ancient Egyptians were much more concerned about the state of their souls after death and made elaborate preparations for the care of their bodies in mummified form. Even today, 3,500 years later, as the sands and tombs of Egypt give up their mummies, the embalmed bodies are found remarkably preserved, awaiting the day, as the Egyptians believed, when the souls would return to them. Not only were their bodies preserved, but the physical forms of their sacred animals—lions, dogs, crocodiles, birds, fishes, and even insects—were also mummified in readiness for the expected resurrection and the renewal of life in some future time in the service of their owners.

We, in this much later day, are amazed and amused at this practice, but it nevertheless demonstrates that the Egyptians held a profound conviction that the soul survived in some separate form, even though they felt that this same soul might again require the use of its earth body.

While mummifying is a lost art, there is much modern embalming and the widespread belief among many that a physical resurrection will one day take place "at the sounding of a trumpet." Just why such believing humans would wish to return, in many instances, to their old worn-out and broken physical forms, if such resurrection were possible, is difficult to conjecture. Consider the millions of children who have died in infancy and the untold millions of young people and adults of all ages, with all the varying types, sizes, and shapes of physical bodies they have occupied, and the colossal confusion attendant upon a sudden restoring of these forms to the state they were at the time of demise! Even if all of them, by some stupendous miracle, were rendered perfect physical specimens, the number of such humans then suddenly alive on this planet would pile flesh mountains high. And what would such a mighty host of humans, so resurrected, do with their newly found life in terms of food and shelter and worthwhile activities and interests?

It is clearly evident to all who dare to think that this earth was not designed as the habitat of the soul after it leaves the physical body.

The Greeks had a different concept concerning the status of the soul after death. They believed in a dim, shadowy place known as Hades which was the abode of the dead. Good and evil souls alike went to Hades, being ferried across the River Styx. There, the souls of the good finally managed to reach the Elysian Fields, a paradise for those deserving special reward, while the wicked were relegated to a deep pit under Hades and forced to dwell in eternal torment. According to further Greek mythology, only those receiving proper burial were allowed to cross the River Styx. If a body remained unburied, its shade was compelled to wander on the bank for one hundred years before crossing.

It is worth observing that the Greeks, in keeping with the Egyptians and many other ancient races, conceived of the soul as existing independent of the body.

Pythagoras, the Greek philosopher, believed in the "transmigration of the soul," namely, that when a human dies his soul passes into the body of another man or animal or even a plant. A dog once howled and Pythagoras is said to have remarked: "It is the soul of a friend of mine. I recognize him by his voice."

Buddha taught the philosophy of transmigration and his followers never kill animals nor take life of any sort. They believe that existence is in itself evil and that the soul lives in many bodies on earth, first in one person and then in another, occasionally in an animal, insect, or plant, rising higher in the scale after every good life and sinking lower with each evil one.

This is similar to the religion of the Hindus who are kind to all living things and persons in the belief that they may possess the souls of some friend or relative who has reincarnated. According to the Hindus, every act in a present life has been conditioned by some act in a past life, human creatures being ruled inexorably by cause and effect. They can only hope to escape from the wheel of life by expiating their karma through performing a good deed for an evil one until all evil has been banished. When this has at last been accomplished, salvation is achieved.

Confucius, great spiritual leader of China, is one who did not deal with the soul as having an existence apart from the body. He stressed the value of men bettering themselves in this life, admonishing them to be honest, faithful, upright, and obedient. Living five hundred years before Christ, one of the Chinese philosopher's famous golden rules was, "What ye would not that others should do unto you, do ye not unto them."

But all spiritual teachers in all ages have emphasized the reward of goodness, either here or hereafter. To live a good life, in most religions, leads to possible salvation through faith and a preferred position of the soul in the next existence.

What, then *is* the soul?

Is it a willowy wraith, a shadowy wisp, a vague shape, a gray mist-like figure, a faint unearthly reflection of the original body form with the seeming awareness of identity?

Or is it just a state of consciousness without form—the intelligence, personality, identity of the individual existing in some dimension incomprehensible to us here?

Or is it the identity plus the life record of the individual, which has no power of its own and knows nothing until called forth by an act of God at the time of the resurrection?

Or is it a higher vibrating, invisible type of physical body, having a recognizable likeness, in which the intelligent entity resides and which enables it to live in a world as real to it there as this world once was?

Is the soul all or any or none of these things?

Has anyone ever really seen a soul?

Can it be scientifically proved that the soul exists?

Scientists and investigators today are approaching the answers to these questions. For instance, Dr. J. B. Rhine, director of the FRNM Foundation, Durham, North Carolina, believes that the existence of a soul has already been scientifically proved and evidence thus points to the survival of personality after death. He and his researchers have demonstrated the fact of telepathy, clairvoyance, and direct control of matter by mental forces. Other scientists, of equal reputation, conducting similar experiments in the field of extrasensory perception, support the findings of Dr. Rhine and his staff.

Discovery that man, as Dr. Rhine states, "is something more than a physical being . . . that an extraphysical factor exists in man ... and that he possesses a non-physical system which can function independent of the physical body," confirms the most basic of all religious doctrines, namely, that man has a spiritual nature. "Insofar as we have gone, research offers a positive suggestion in favor of survival."

I have followed the research of outstanding scientists in this field with profound interest, for my own life has been privately devoted to personal investigation, experimentation, and study with respect to the great mystery of human consciousness and its possible survival after death. I learned much about the operation of higher powers of mind in my intensive long-distance telepathic tests conducted with Sir Hubert Wilkins, Arctic explorer, under conditions set by Dr. Gardner Murphy, then head of the Parapsychology Department at Columbia University.

I make reference to this only to indicate to you, who may not have been familiar with the Wilkins-Sherman experiments, that I speak from personal experience and that I have devoted a lifetime to training and self-discipline that I might be enabled to judge and evaluate "things not seen" which are *contactable* only through the developed and more sensitized higher faculties of mind and soul.

I ask you to accept, then, the statements I have made and will make in this book as being the result of honest and fearless research. I am sure you will appreciate that it has not been easy for me, nor would it have been for you, to have put aside all preconceived ideas of religion, philosophy, and the supposed material nature of this world in order to maintain an open mind in the pursuit of this most elusive self-knowledge, so that I might, if possible, prove, for myself at least, whether or not higher powers of consciousness really did exist, whether or not man possessed a soul, and, if so, whether or not that soul survived death.

My testimony, therefore, must be largely personal in nature, based not upon hearsay or supposition but upon my own convictions after years of concentrated study, investigation, and reflection. You can depend upon it that what I do not know I will freely confess. What seems to be true, as the result of my personal experience, I will frankly state. What is only a theory or a deduction at the present time, I will also declare.

But I say to you, now, in advance of such evidence as I hope to present, that I am convinced:

(1) That man possesses higher or spiritual powers of mind which can be developed by conscious effort;

(2) that man possesses a soul, an ego, an identity which survives death;

(3) that man possesses a spirit form as well as a physical body which this soul occupies at death;

(4) that the next existence is as real and as rational as this one;

(5) that we take over into the next life only that which we have developed in consciousness here;

(6) that, in consideration of these facts, our entire system of education, religious thinking, moral training, and daily living will need to be drastically changed to permit the fullest development of the soul in preparation for the life to come.

In support of the above premises, the contents of this book are dedicated.

It should be obvious to you, at the outset, that if science proves man's survival after death, irrespective of any religious faith, this mighty truth should bring about a unification of all religions and do away with the alleged necessity for special beliefs, baptisms, rituals, and the entire man-made machinery of salvation. Man will then stand forth as a creature possessing not only free will and free choice but a free soul—freed, at last, of all false concepts and fears of eternal punishment.

But this freedom will impose upon him the individual responsibility of developing his own soul through right thinking and living in order that he may earn the rewards reserved for those who have prepared themselves, knowingly and faithfully, for the greater experience awaiting them after death. Christ's real purpose on earth will then be revealed and more emphasis will be placed upon the life He lived than upon His death. As the Way-Shower, Christ demonstrated in his exemplary life the spiritual principles by which all "sons of God," His brothers, should live. He constantly stressed the value of the soul, but we, even today, have not begun to comprehend just how priceless our possession of a soul really is.

When you consider that the soul is that part of you which survives death, you are now better able to appreciate the full significance of Christ's declaration: "For what shall it profit a man, if he shall gain the whole world, and lose his own soul?" (Mark 8-36), and his further admonition: "And fear not them which kill the body, but are not able to kill the soul . . ." (Matthew 10-28).

With His spiritual understanding, Christ knew, as all true spiritual leaders knew before Him and have known after Him, that development of soul qualities through right thinking and adherence to the spiritual laws of the universe should be man's primary objective in life. He told us, "In my Father's house are many mansions. . . . I go to prepare a place for you . . . that where I am ye may be also . . ." (John 14-2,3), implying that the next existence was a definite state of being in time and space and that, in fact, there were many states (mansions) in the hereafter. He was giving us more specific information because of his spiritually attained knowledge and perceptions than we have recognized even up to the present day.

He knew that every human who paid little or no heed to soul development was handicapping himself severely in the life to come. In fact, the only "hell" we suffer on this earth or hereafter is due to our lack of soul development and the consequent ills and limitations which this lack has brought, is bringing, and will bring upon us.

Had Christ not lived such a good life in accordance with spiritual principles, His death on the cross would have meant nothing to mankind. Thieves and other offenders were often dispatched in this manner, their lives being considered of so little worth that we have no record of their deaths save those two who were hanged beside Christ. And, even here, Christ is reported to have said to one of them: "Today shalt thou be with me in Paradise" (Luke 23-43). Once more this Great Teacher was giving evidence of His conviction that there was a state after death to which all humans were destined. He had gained a conscious awareness of this state through His highly developed spiritual senses. He was then able to face death fearlessly, with the sublime faith based upon actual personal knowledge that He would live again in a higher state of being, and that all fellow humans would likewise survive, gravitating to that plane of existence which their soul development warranted.

What would *you* give to possess this same inner knowledge and faith in the face of death?

Life is so ordered that we can gain actual knowledge of the world without and within only through personal experience. We must make direct contact with a thing, a subject, or a person if we would really know that thing or subject or person. In the same way, but in a higher sense, we must be able to make contact with our own individual intelligence, ego, or soul by developed methods of meditation, concentration, and reflection to gain a conscious awareness and growing knowledge of our own real self, and through this knowledge an evolving understanding of our spiritual relationship to that great intelligence of which we are a part.

Unhappily, man's failure to give more thought and attention to development of his inner spiritual powers has been due, mainly, to false concepts and misguided teachings. He has remained, for the most part, ignorant of the wondrous powers inherent in all humans, which only await self-discovery to be demonstrated. Millions have been brought up in the belief that they were created in sin and thus had no power in and of themselves to rise above evil. Lacking this power, as they thought, they naturally had no incentive to try to improve their natures. They felt that salvation of their souls depended on a force outside themselves, exercised by God solely in response to an act of faith.

The magnetic and vitalizing power of faith is not to be minimized, but man has erred in believing that faith *alone* is sufficient. He has been told that "faith without works is dead" (James 2-17,) and many spiritual leaders and philosophers have emphasized the necessity for man to put forth an individual effort to improve the quality and character of his own soul as a means of insuring a happier existence here and hereafter. That mankind has largely neglected this practice is due to the fact that salvation has been offered to the sinner without requirement for self-development, simply in return for a confession of penitence and a profession of faith.

Had humans fully realized what spiritual rewards they could have earned for themselves by daily concentration on the development of their own higher powers of consciousness while on earth, the entire mass level of mankind would have long since been lifted to the threshold of true, universal brotherhood. Had organized religion, in itself, possessed the power to purify men's souls, this would have been achieved centuries ago. But the tragic fact remains that the souls of men are just as filled with evil, hatred, prejudice, and lust today as they were in olden times, clearly indicating that all true spiritual development can come only from *within*.

Until each man is inspired by his religion or by a revealing personal experience to seek self-development, there will be no improvement of his soul quality and no spiritual advancement of civilization.

But how do you personally know that you possess a soul? What evidence do you have?

Perhaps none, now. Perhaps you have only accepted the fact that you possess a soul on faith. But underneath it all, in moments of serious contemplation of the future, you, no doubt, would like to know for a certainty that you have a soul and that it actually does survive death.

This knowledge and inner assurance will come to you as and when you learn how to make your mind receptive, so that the higher powers within you can function. Once this happens, you will share with others the inspired awareness that you are more than mortal, that you have a physical body and a spiritual body and that you, at present, dwell in both these bodies at one and the same time! You will realize that your soul, as such, cannot be seen because it, as the real you, must always clothe itself in form. This will be true throughout all eternity because intelligence requires form in and through which to manifest itself. And each type and degree of intelligence reproduces itself in a form adapted to whatever plane of life on which it then functions.

That man possesses a soul can no longer be scientifically denied by those who have made a fair and unbiased investigation of mental phenomena and have gained first-hand evidence of their soul's actual existence. Your soul, right now, possesses in potentiality all that you will ever hope for or can be. It has the God-given power to attract to you all manner of conditions and circumstances which are needed to accomplish any result you desire within the range of your physical, mental, and spiritual resources. This being true, you can commence to comprehend how important it is for you—and every human—to get thoroughly acquainted with your own soul.

3. EVIDENCES OF A SPIRIT BODY

MY PROFOUND INTEREST in the mysteries of life and death was born of a tragic experience in our own home when I was a boy of sixteen. At that time, my beloved brother Edward, aged eleven, fell from a tree in our front yard and was so severely injured that he died a week later after terrible suffering.

His death was the first break in our family circle. I was left numb with a grief that I could not fully comprehend, and more than that, I was left with a feeling of agonizing uncertainty concerning God. If He was the Giver and the Taker of life, why had He visited this suffering and death on an innocent boy like Edward? Many criminals and godless humans had never been caused such pain.

Why? Why? Why?

At the funeral service there was the usual spiritual consolation; "It is hard for us to understand why a tragedy such as this should befall one we hold dear. But our wisdom is not God's and He has seen fit to call this soul home."

A strange resentment and rebellion stirred within me. If this were true, if an Infinite Being, the God of this universe whom I'd been taught to believe was all-merciful and just, had decreed that my brother Edward should fall from a tree and break his arms and contract blood poisoning and suffer a week of unspeakable agony, then to die

. . . if God had had any hand in this, then He was not the kind of God I would worship.

Well-intentioned religious folk said to Mother that some day she would understand, that this experience was a test of faith. If so, what a cruel, inhuman, and undeserved test! Did my brother have to suffer and die to satisfy a God that my parents really believed in Him and were subservient to His will?

This idea violated all reason. And yet, ordinarily straight-thinking people were placing this interpretation upon the tragedy. Or *did* people think straight when it came to religion?

I determined to find out for myself in my own mind and in my own way. After Edward's demise, I became interested in all forms of mental phenomena. I found little solace in the learned books on religions and philosophies. They were filled, for the most part, with spiritual platitudes which made nice reading but left me unconvinced.

God, to me, defied finite comprehension. He was a synonym for a creative intelligence embodying time, space, eternity, and all the universal elements, whatever they might be. Even this was totally inadequate—it was futile to attempt a definition.

But it was clear to me that the God of an inconceivably vast universe would not favor any part of His creation. Therefore, no human beings could have an "inside track" to God with any of their interpretations. And anyone who claimed to have might be sincere in his contention but be self-deluded or misguided.

I wanted to know the truth, not someone else's interpretation of it. And, more and more, I was impressed by the growing conviction that the only way we could ever come to solve the mysteries of life was through an exploration of human consciousness. The answer was to be found not outside of man, but *in his stream of consciousness*.

What was in that stream? Everything, seemingly!

But how were the various levels of the stream of consciousness to be sounded and tapped?

This was the problem; it had been the problem for centuries. But forces of nature had been harnessed by man. Why not, eventually, the mysterious and wonderful forces of mind? And if mind contained the spiritual or higher mental powers accorded to it by the wise men of all ages, then it should be possible for these powers to be demonstrated. Muscles of the body could be developed through persistent exercise. Why not our higher mental faculties, once the laws through which they operated were uncovered and applied?

Man had always been a mystery to his own self. He used forces he didn't understand or try to understand because he found they worked. And he called what he *didn't* understand "the works of God" and what he *did* understand, "the handiwork of man."

Even today, with all the marvelous advances of science and invention, man was in just as great darkness concerning his own origin, the operation of his mind, and his relation to the universe as he had ever been. But he was given the ability to know as much about the expression of the life he found himself in as he needed to know. The only limitation was that which man placed upon himself through ignorance or unwillingness to learn.

And who could foretell? Perhaps back of the human mind there existed the real, true revelation of the nature and character of God—the answer to the riddles of the universe!

This was too ambitious a picture for any one or a million persons to attempt to bring forth. But a start had to be made. There was an urge in me, a something deep down within, that had to be satisfied.

My hobby, through life, would be a study of mental phenomena. I would keep an open mind on all things, as free of prejudice and preconceived ideas as humanly possible. I would experiment and observe and then make my deductions. And someday there might be crystallized, in my own mind at least, a faith based upon demonstrable truth . . . a faith that would serve me throughout life in a practical, everyday way.

It was in the fall of 1917 that I was operated upon for

appendicitis at the Battle Creek Sanitarium. The nurse assigned to me was a middle-aged man by the name of David N. H. Quinn.

I became impressed, almost at once, that here was no ordinary human being. Soft of voice and manner, Mr. Quinn's eyes had an unusual *knowing* quality about them. My slightest need was anticipated without my speaking a word. At first I thought this simply the ministrations of an excellent nurse. But one night something happened which made me wonder.

The commissary building, next to the hospital, caught fire. It was a general alarm blaze and there was mad excitement outside and in. Nurses had their hands full calming nervous patients and moving others from the wing nearest the burning storehouse. David Quinn was off duty and I was in bed in my room, unable to get up, with the reflection from the flames dancing on the ceiling.

I had no fear, just a strong desire to see the fire. Oh, if only David were here to lift me and carry me to the window and seat me on the ledge, so that I could look out!

As more and more fire trucks arrived and the fire mounted so that my room was light as day, my desire to see what was going on became intensified. I had raised myself up on an elbow and was staring toward the window when I heard footsteps. It was David. He came in, smiling, and bent over me.

"Put your arms around my neck," he instructed.

I did so and David took a firm grip under me. I was lifted like a babe and transported to the window. David slid it up and rested me against the sill, in position so that I could get a good view of the blaze.

"This is against hospital regulations," he said, still smiling. "But I'm sure it won't hurt you . . . and this is what you wanted, isn't it?"

"Yes," I nodded, and gazed at him, wonderingly. "But how did you know?"

"I have a way of knowing things," he said, and this was all I could get out of him.

But a strong friendship sprang up between David and me. He seemed to be unmindful of the difference in ages.

And he was the first person I had met to whom I could talk about my mental searchings with the feeling that he understood. It was as thrilling as it was helpful.

David had a deep belief in the power of mind. To him, communication between minds was an established fact. He told me that telepathy was only a conscious development of what we called our "intuition." When we felt that certain things were so, or had happened, and this was later proved to have been correct, it was our telepathic faculty that had been operating. But most of us had refused to accept this explanation and had dismissed the evidence on the basis of chance or coincidence.

"It's coming, though," David predicted. "You'll live to see these higher powers of mind demonstrated and recognized by science."

I returned home to Traverse City, Michigan, for convalescence but kept in touch with David by correspondence. His letters indicated an amazing, intimate knowledge of my activities and he gave me advice as though he were actually present.

Late in 1918, after I had gone into the service and had changed addresses several times, I lost contact with David. He had left the sanitarium and, when last heard from, had been at a health resort in the Adirondacks, caring for a wealthy patient. He had mailed me a book from there, entitled *The Diary of Jean Evarts,* by Charles Francis Stocking, which had to do with the powers of mind, in which he knew I would be interested. My letter thanking him for this book was returned, marked "No forwarding address."

With the war over, I was back in Traverse City in January of 1919. David had been out of my mind for some weeks, when an astonishing thing happened.

I awakened the night of the nineteenth, around one o'clock with the strange feeling that I was paralyzed and could not move a muscle. Looking up, in the semidarkness of my room, I was shocked to see David. In life size, standing beside the bed. He was staring down at me with a fixed expression, full of yearning. I sensed at once that there was something he very much wanted to tell me. But I was panicky from the realization of his apparent presence and the fact that I couldn't move. I struggled mentally to extricate myself and saw a look of disappointment on David's face. He faded from sight as I recovered the use of my body.

This was an entirely new kind of experience and I lay wondering if it had been a realistic dream. It was hard for me to determine, now that the phenomenon was over, what had really taken place. It seemed impossible that I had actually seen David's form and face, yet there had been enough reflection from the all-night light in the upstairs hall to enable me to make out dimly all the familiar objects in my room and prevent me from conjuring up an image out of them. There seemed no reason existing within myself why I should suddenly have awakened, out of a sound sleep, to find David, startlingly lifelike, standing beside my bed.

Could he be seriously ill or in trouble of some kind? I asked myself.

It was some hours before I could drop off to sleep again. With the morning, and further opportunity for consideration, I decided that I must have had a vivid dream experience which stayed with me at the moment of waking and almost carried over into my conscious state. Perhaps David had been thinking strongly of me and was writing.

But on the next night, at precisely the same time, I was awakened again, once more unable to move—and with David again standing at my side.

I was more prepared for such an occurrence this time, but, even so, it was a shock. I was sure now that David was undergoing a great crisis of some kind and I tried to speak to him.

"David!" I cried.

And his figure, with an earnest, almost anguished look on his face, merged into the shadows of the room.

Getting up and turning on the light, I decided to write a letter, sending it to David's last-known address, in hope that this time it would reach him. In this letter I related my two uncanny experiences and urged David to get in touch with me, expressing concern for his health and safety. The following morning, when the letter had been dispatched, I felt better.

I told Mother and Dad of what had happened at breakfast. They listened with respectful interest but had no explanation to offer.

I went to bed the night of January twenty-first with not the slightest thought that the experience would be repeated. I must have dropped off to sleep almost immediately. But I came to as the town clock was striking the hour of one as though I had been touched on the face.

There, bending over me, was David Quinn. His lips seemed to be moving, and I tried now, with every nerve and fiber of my body, to hear or discern what he was trying to say. No sounds came from those moving lips but there was a look of love and concern and intentness in the eyes.

Why couldn't I sense what he wished to tell me?

"Oh, David! David!" I cried inwardly. And I finally got control of my hands and reached out toward him with both arms.

His form eluded me. It seemed to take on a distant quality and there came over me the terrible sensation that David was leaving me forever, as though I had rushed down to a pier from which an ocean liner was departing, only to have arrived too late. Up on deck was the form of the friend I had come to see off. He was waving at me with an expression of infinite sadness upon his face. There was too great a distance between us as the liner swung out into the stream and the blackness of the night for him to shout a message. What he might have said to me could never more be said. He was smiling across a body of water from which there could be no return.

"David! David!" I now cried out, so that I heard the sound of my own voice.

I was sitting up in bed, staring at his figure, fading slowly . . . seeming to grow stronger for an instant . . . then fading again . . . his eyes fixed upon me.

And now he was gone and I was up and had the light on and was pacing about my room.

No, I hadn't been dreaming. No one could tell me that. I had no witnesses to this experience, but anyone interested would have to take my word for it.

I had *seen* David Quinn! I didn't know anything about the properties of ghosts or apparitions or what explanation there might be, if any—but I had seen David Quinn!

He had been in my room, in Traverse City, Michigan, just a few minutes before. He had visited me, awakening me from sleep, on three consecutive nights!

The first night . . . the second night—a dream, possibly. But this *third* night, most vivid and realistic of all! What could be the matter? Why had David seemed to be trying so persistently to speak to me? How could I find out where he was?

This time I knew, an inner something told me, that he would not return again. His departure had the finality of a last farewell about it.

Three weeks passed, with no word from David. But my letter, addressed to him, was returned.

Then, one late afternoon in February, I came home to find two letters in the box, both from Battle Creek friends of David. One was from Victor Bjork, with whom I had formerly roomed at the sanitarium; the other was from a nurse, Miss Isobel Macheracker,* whom I barely knew.

Both letters had been written for the purpose of informing me of David Quinn's death on the night of *January twenty-first,* in Brooklyn's Long Island College hospital. He had been in the East on a case and the influenza epidemic had caught him. Removed to the hospital, his illness developed into double pneumonia. He died *after having been in a coma for three days!*

But the most startling point of this information was a statement made by Miss Macheracker. "It's strange," she wrote, "but on each of the three nights prior to David's passing, he appeared at my bedside. I knew he was in trouble and was calling to me and I'd have gone to him at once if I'd only known where he was."

* Dr. Isobel Macheracker, as this is written, is still living and resides in Kansas City, Missouri.

Here was confirming evidence of my own experience! Here was *proof* it had not been a dream! Miss Macheracker, miles away in Battle Creek, and I, up in Traverse City, had had *identical* experiences!

Allowing for a difference in time between Brooklyn and our locations in Michigan, David had passed away early in the morning of January twenty-first, at almost precisely the moment we had apparently seen him on the three successive nights!

What was the answer?

I was baffled. I didn't pretend to know. I would have to learn much more about these things before I could even hazard a guess.

I have always had a habit of stretching out on the cot in my study when I am doing creative work, relaxing and dropping off to sleep for a few minutes, then awakening refreshed and going back to the typewriter, resuming where I have left off.

One particular afternoon, some years after the death of David Quinn, I awakened with a start to hear my wife Martha, who had been out shopping, about to enter the apartment, keys rattling in the door. My small daughter Mary was with her, and because Martha usually had her arms full of bundles, it had been my practice to go to the door and let her in.

This time, as I exerted the will to get up, my physical body seemed paralyzed. But *something* in me *did* respond, for I suddenly found myself bumping up against the closed door of my study!

I had no consciousness of being in a body or having form, at the door, but I was shocked as I looked back and saw my physical body lying on the cot!

This was a totally new experience and it frightened me. I relinquished my intent to go to the door and suddenly discovered myself back in my physical body, struggling to gain control of it.

Again there was the sound of keys in the lock, and once more I tried to respond, only to have this same phenomenon occur! I was out of my body, at the door of my room. I hit up against it with a strange, mentally bruising force.

I saw my body on the cot and this sensation was so terrifying that I abandoned my urge to answer the door with one thought in mind: to return to the body. This time I succeeded and was relieved to find I could move.

But now I heard Martha coming down the hall, with Mary running ahead of her into the living room and snapping on the radio. On came a jazz orchestra selection.

I rose to a sitting position and got unsteadily to my feet. My mind seemed somewhat dazed, but, as it cleared, I was startled by a sudden realization:

Martha and Mary weren't in the apartment!
They hadn't come home yet!
The radio was not on!

While I was standing, trying to figure this out, I actually *did* hear the keys in the lock. I was too astounded to move.

Now Mary was running down the hall. I could hear the patter of her feet.

Snap! There went the radio on, bringing in the very orchestra selection I had heard a few moments before!

This entire scene had taken place in my consciousness before it had really happened!

What strange prank had *time* played upon me? What had really happened when I appeared to have left my body? Had an inner part of me actually detached itself, momentarily, from the physical? Why had I been stopped at the door of my room, unable to get beyond it? Could this have been due to my mental concept that I could not pass through a door without opening it? Was it because I had always considered my body as *me?* And now that I was *outside* my body, amazed to find I was existing in some other form, was the experience so new that my mind could not readily adapt itself to these changed conditions and restricted my movements as though I were still in the physical body?

What dimension had I been in, anyway, that I could sense a happening before it had actually taken place? What conditions had brought about this entire experience, uninvited?

I had no logical answers at that time. It required years

of further experimentation and observation before I felt qualified to draw certain specific conclusions. And, during this interim, other experiences came to me, each casting its glimmer of light on what had been experienced before.

One incident was particularly significant and deserves a chapter by itself.

4. A VERIFIED CASE OF PROJECTION OF THE PSYCHE

THE LITERATURE of the occult and the Far East, especially, is filled with accounts of so-called "Astral travel." It tells of purported "masters" who have attained such high mental and spiritual development that they can leave their physical bodies at will and travel to distant points on earth.

In most instances, adepts possessing this ability are said to be conscious of their visitations, appearing before either friends or strangers, according to inclination or mission, and engaging in conversation or not, as they choose. Such powers have been particularly accredited to members of high-caste Indian or Tibetan peoples. We are told of the different Yogi practices and methods of self-denial, self-discipline, consecration, and concentration which various masters have employed to attain their great development.

To those of us in the Western World, these accounts of the psychic accomplishments of advanced souls often make exciting and impressive reading. Many of us have delved into occult lore with the same spirit and interest that we would show in a good mystery story. Very interesting if true, but of course we don't believe it. We laugh at any of our friends who are taking this psychic stuff seriously. In our opinion there is nothing authentic in any of these reported phenomena, and the idea of any human leaving his body and transporting himself by some secret method of spiritual jet propulsion is too ridiculous for words.

We are almost totally ignorant, of course, of what is actually taking place, or can take place, in the realm of the mind. We have a working knowledge of how the motor in our automobile functions but lack a true understanding of our own selves and cannot explain how our minds operate. But we have a right to be skeptical, since our own common sense tells us that many of our friends who believe in the occult are gullible, wishful-thinking, self-deluded, emotionally unbalanced, fanatically religious, and ism-devoted individuals. Their unquestioning acceptance of everything they read or hear along psychic lines causes us to lose respect for their judgment and to decide that we want no part of this occult business if this is the effect it has upon those who become involved in it.

Tibet is a long way from our geographical location and we can see no beneficial human purposes served by these spiritual hermits who remain aloof from the world and meditate upon the life of the spirit. From the standpoint of our logic, it seems that we would not have been born *into* this world if we had been supposed to live *out* of it. We see no value whatsoever in mortifying the flesh or contemplating our navel to become one with God.

One of the great drawbacks to the serious interest we might otherwise take in psychic happenings has been the criminal chicanery and fraudulent practices existing in this spiritual field. It has been and still is honeycombed with fake spirit mediums, dishonest spiritual leaders, misguided cultists and psychic teachers who have flooded the world with deliberate misinformation, imaginative flights of fancy, untrue representations and trick performances of telepathy, clairvoyance, prophecy, spirit communication, spirit materialization, trumpet sittings, automatic writing, psychic reading, fortune-telling, and every other form of occult divination.

To recognize and to rescue the genuine mental and spiritual faculties from this wilderness is a task for the experienced investigator, not for the well-meaning tyro who can be easily deceived by a sincere but self-deluded friend. It is a difficult and often thankless job to weed out the perpetrators of conscious and unconscious frauds from those possessing and demonstrating actual evidence of developed extrasensory perceptive powers.

In my own investigation of mental phenomena, I have made it a rule not to depend upon hearsay but to rely on personal experience and observation only, as a means of approaching the truth. While I have long believed in the existence of deeper mental faculties in man, it has been necessary to maintain an attitude of open-minded skepticism in considering each new purported instance of such phenomena. Often the individual who thinks he has demonstrated, either consciously or unconsciously, the power of telepathy, clairvoyance, or precognition, is a highly imaginative, excitable, emotional, or undependable type who has not the ability to marshal his facts logically and to discriminate between a coincidence or chance happening and other factors which would explain away his experience.

Each reported case must be carefully investigated by a competent researcher in order to determine its authenticity. Yet in the face of this ever-present difficulty, there is on file with the English and American Psychical Research Societies and other accredited investigative groups literally thousands of carefully checked cases of such phenomena covering every phase of this profound subject, the surface of which has barely been touched.

We do not have to go as far afield as Tibet to get evidence of the ability of the soul of man, under certain conditions, to leave the body and to impress upon the mind or sight of a person, or persons, at a distance, sometimes thousands of miles away, the recognizable image and occasionally the voice of that personality. Moreover, most of these case histories have to do with individuals who make no claim to self-mastery or practice of Yoga or any other occult method. They are, for the most part, run-of-the-mill men and women of all ages and classes who, under different emotional stresses or while deeply desirous of seeing some distant person or place, have left their body, either in a sleeping or waking state, and appeared before that person or at the place they had in mind.

This kind of phenomenon, as incredible as it might seem to you, has happened enough times and been observed and experienced by enough people so that there is no longer any doubt of its actual occurrence. My own experiences, as previously related, and others of a similar nature, which serve no purpose in recounting here, had convinced me that the soul could project itself in time and space.

I was to have further startling proof of this fact on Thanksgiving Day, 1941, while residing at the Canterbury Apartments in Hollywood, California. I had come to know a remarkable human being who then lived in Monterey Park, between fifteen and twenty miles from Hollywood on the other side of Los Angeles. His name was Harry J. Loose. He had served as a policeman on the Chicago police force, later as a plainclothes man assigned to Hull House, and finally, acting as a private detective, he ended his career as head of the police staff at the *Chicago Daily News* from which he retired in 1934 and moved to California.

In the days of the Redpath Chautauqua, Mr. Loose was a nationally recognized authority, speaking on the subject of crime and criminology, but few of his friends were aware that Harry J. Loose was a highly developed man mentally who possessed and could demonstrate, at will, unusual mental faculties. Because of our mutual interest in this subject, we were drawn closely together. While I was in Hollywood on a picture-writing assignment, I considered it much to my benefit to hold Sunday afternoons open so that Mrs. Sherman and I could spend them either at the Loose home or with the Looses at our apartment.

We learned much in discussions with this rare individual, not only of the higher states of mind but of the nature and character of the universe and what happened after the change called death. Mr. Loose, as the result of severe injuries sustained in police work, was afflicted with serious heart trouble. He was not the least concerned, however, with the thought that his time on earth might be comparatively short. He was as positive of a life after death as the average human is that there is going to be a tomorrow. He stated to us that he had been on "the other side" quite a number of times and thus knew what conditions he would encounter when physical death occurred and that the sensation of being freed of this earthly body was wonderful beyond description.

In appreciation of this valued friendship and the fine interest of Harry Loose in us, my wife and I had a Thanksgiving basket of fruit sent to the Loose home. We had our standing date to see the Looses in Monterey Park that coming Sunday, so were surprised, upon returning from a short drive about three P.M. Thanksgiving afternoon, to find a memorandum slip in our box at the Canterbury, timed at two-thirty P.M. and filled out by Mr. Cousins, the desk clerk on duty, which read: "Mr. Loose was here—will see you on Sunday."

We instantly regretted our absence from the apartment since, in Mr. Loose's physical condition, the drive to Hollywood through downtown Los Angeles traffic was always fatiguing, especially on a holiday. We were amazed to think that he would have made the long trip on the chance of finding us in and that he had not telephoned to tell us of his coming. This was in the days before freeways.

Because it customarily took us about an hour to drive to the Loose home in Monterey Park, we figured, since he reportedly had been at the Canterbury only half an hour earlier, that he would still not have arrived back at his own address. We decided, therefore, to wait a few minutes before phoning to express our regrets at having been out when he had called.

At about three-thirty we put the call through and Harry answered immediately. I thanked him for making the long drive to see us and told him how sorry we were not to have been home. There was a hesitation on the phone, and then Harry said concernedly: "Harold, there's been some mistake. You have me confused with someone else. I didn't come to see you. I haven't been out of the house today."

This was surprising information. I looked down at the

memorandum slip in my hand. It plainly stated that, "Mr. Loose was here. . . ." The "Mr. Loose" was spelled correctly.

"That's very strange," I replied. "Your name is recorded saying you had called in person and that you would see us on Sunday."

"That's right," replied Harry. "I'm expecting you folks over here this Sunday but I repeat, Harold, your man at the desk has made a mistake. Josie and Ray and little John* were here for Thanksgiving dinner. I haven't even had my shoes on all day. I'm dressed in my work pants and the old brown sweater and slippers you've usually seen me wearing here at home. And my car hasn't been out of the garage."

"That's funny," said I. "I can't figure out how Mr. Cousins could have made such an error. In the first place, he's never met you because he doesn't work Sundays—the only day you ever come over here. I can't imagine how he'd get your name. Well, anyhow, we'll be seeing you Sunday."

I hung up and went immediately downstairs to check the memorandum with Mr. Cousins. I told him that the party he had listed as calling on us had just advised me on the phone that he hadn't been out of the house all day. I asked if he remembered the man well enough to describe his appearance. He said that he did, that the gentleman looked like a working man, that he wore working pants, a brown sweater with dark blue shirt, and that he had a cap on.

I was astounded at the accurate description. Mr. Cousins, noting my perplexity, asked: "What's the matter?"

"Something's very odd," I replied. "You've described Mr. Loose perfectly and just as he says he has been dressed today."

Mr. Cousins was now the one to be astounded. "That's peculiar," he said. "Now that you tell me that, I recall several unusual things about this man. I looked up and saw him standing at the desk, not having noticed him come in.

---

* Mr. Loose's daughter, son-in-law, and grandson.

He gave me this message for you, speaking slowly and with great difficulty, as though he had false teeth and was having trouble keeping them in place. He spoke clearly, however, and wanted to know, after I'd written down his message, if I had it correct. There was a woman guest at the desk at the time, and she commented after he left about his being 'a strange person'." Mr. Cousins looked at me with sudden interest. "But, Mr. Sherman," he continued, "if this wasn't Mr. Loose, who was it?"

"That's a question I can't answer right now," I said. "I'll have to report to you later."

Hurrying back to our apartment, I put in another call to Mr. Loose. Getting him on the wire, I said: "Harry, I've just talked with Mr. Cousins and he has given me an accurate description of you—so accurate that it could not have been anyone else. I'm completely mystified. What do you make of it?"

The tone in Harry's voice was extremely sober. "I don't exactly know," he said. "If Mr. Cousins has described my appearance exactly, as you say, then he must have seen something. I've never had an experience just like this before. It disturbs me greatly. I don't want to discuss it on the phone but I'll talk to you about it when we meet on Sunday. Meanwhile, I suggest that you don't make anything of this to Mr. Cousins until I can get some kind of light on what actually took place."

We could hardly wait until Sunday afternoon and our regularly scheduled visit at the Loose home. Harry was wearing the same clothes he had worn Thanksgiving Day, his customary apparel about the house and yard. On Sundays, when he had come to visit us, he had never worn these clothes but had put on what he called his "one Sunday suit" for these occasions.

We had never seen Harry with such a serious mien as he had that day. As we sat in his modest living room, he said to me: "Harold, I think the time has come when I must tell you a few things about myself that I was afraid you would not understand and believe. For some years now I have had the ability to leave my body and consciously to appear in spirit form at distant places on visits to certain individuals. During the time I am absent from my physical body, it remains in a deep sleep state and is cared for by Mother Loose. If I am gone in the daytime and should neighbors drop in, she simply explains, having closed off the bedroom, that Harry is sleeping and can't be disturbed. To try to arouse me during those periods would be a great nervous shock. I may tell you that one of the friends I meet in this manner is a John Carlos, a highly developed Catholic priest who lives in South America. At times he visits me in the same manner. I myself am not Catholic, as you know, and this spiritual development has nothing to do with any creed."

Harry paused and we sat deeply enthralled.

"Do you remember, Harold," Harry continued, "how I have liked to walk you down to the little park near here and to sit on a certain bench with you under the pepper tree where we could see the children playing innocently about and the majestic mountains in the distance?"

I nodded. "Yes," I said. "It's a beautiful place."

"It's the place," Harry went on, "where I go to meet John Carlos when he calls on me. We communicate telepathically and when he has something of spiritual importance he wants to discuss, either he or I go to the other. There is much I cannot tell you because spiritual growth and understanding is a matter of development. But if you had been in the park with me and were permitted to share this experience, you would suddenly see another man standing near the bench or seated beside me. To the casual observer, we would look just like two ordinary old men, inconspicuously dressed—such old men as you often see whiling away their time on park benches throughout the country."

As Harry paused again to let the import of what he had said sink in, I recalled the peculiar attachment he seemed to have for this particular section of the park. In the early morning and late afternoon hours it was particularly quiet, inspiring and inviting to meditation. What he had felt compelled to tell us was of enormous interest, but I couldn't help wondering what bearing it could have upon the strange occurrence at the Canterbury.

Harry seemed to sense as much for he continued: "These meetings between John Carlos and myself were always prearranged. Each was expecting the other when he arrived and each was entirely conscious of the visitation, able to return to his physical body and, upon regaining normal consciousness, retain a memory of the experience. But what has greatly concerned me, in the evidence you present of my visitation to the Canterbury, is the fact that I have no recollection whatsoever of such a projection. Though my form is reported to have been seen, and my voice heard delivering an intelligent message, by a man whose integrity and observation are not to be doubted, I would rather believe it had not happened. I want to make absolutely certain that this Mr. Cousins actually saw an image of me and I'd like to drive over to the Canterbury some day soon, dressed exactly as I was that day, and confront him and see if he recognizes me."

"I think that's an excellent idea," I approved. "You name the day and the approximate time. I'll meet you on the corner and we'll go in the side door entrance to the Canterbury lobby. I'll remain just inside the door, looking down the hall, so I'll be able to see you when you reach the desk and stand before Mr. Cousins. It will be impossible for him to see me. If he recognizes you without any suggestion as to who you are, then we both should be convinced that he also saw you on Thanksgiving afternoon."

"That's right," Harry agreed. "I'll drop you a note as soon as I know when I can come."

Accordingly, in the first mail the following Tuesday morning, I received a brief note which read:

Harold:
If it is not a rainy or too threatening day, I expect to be over this coming Tuesday morning as close to 10 as I can make it. . . .

It was a few minutes after ten when, returning from a short shopping trip on Hollywood Boulevard, I saw Harry backing into a parking space half a block down the street.

He got out of the car attired in his familiar yard clothes and accompanied me to the Yucca Street entrance of the Canterbury, around on the side of the apartment house.

I stepped inside the door with him. We could look down the hall, straight past the desk situated in the elbow made by the junction of hall and lobby. We heard Mr. Cousins' voice talking to someone on the telephone. Harry left me, as arranged, and walked down the hall, stopping at the desk and facing the switchboard. Mr. Cousins, of course, and the desk were not visible to me.

Harry did not speak. He simply stood looking at Mr. Cousins, and I suddenly heard the desk clerk's voice call out in a tone of alarm and surprise: "Oh! Good morning, Mr. Loose!"

Harry then replied: "Good morning. Is Mr. Sherman in?"

And I heard Mr. Cousins say: "No, I think he went out just a few minutes ago."

I could tell that Mr. Cousins was actually unnerved, as though he might be seeing another apparition, so I hastened down the hall to allay his fears, smilingly assuring him that this *was* Mr. Loose, in the flesh.

Mr. Cousins gave a sigh of genuine relief. "Well," he said, "I'm glad to know that. I didn't know *what* to think this time!"

But even with this identification, Harry still wasn't satisfied.

"Do you mind repeating for me just what you saw and what I said Thanksgiving day?"

Mr. Cousins complied, giving Harry substantially the same account he had previously related to me.

"But," persisted Harry, "will you please examine me closely. I want to make sure that you actually saw me. Am I dressed as you remember me on Thanksgiving Day?"

Mr. Cousins studied a moment and then replied: "I don't seem to recall that shirt. I believe it's a lighter color than the one you had on the last time I saw you."

Harry nodded. "That's right," he confirmed. "I was wearing a darker blue shirt, which is now in the wash."

Mr. Cousins shook his head, completely puzzled. "This is uncanny," he said. "It gives me goose pimples. Can you explain how it happened?"

Harry hesitated. I could see that he was reluctant to tell Mr. Cousins any more than was absolutely necessary.

"This is a form of mental phenomena which sometimes occurs," he said. "You don't need to worry, Mr. Cousins. It will never happen again. I want to thank you for your cooperation in reporting what you have to Mr. Sherman and identifying me. I hope we'll meet some time again."

He extended his hand, which Mr. Cousins took, replying: "I hope so, too, Mr. Loose—but only in the *flesh!*"

We then took the elevator to my apartment where Harry dropped into a chair, sitting silently and meditating for at least half an hour. He appeared greatly disturbed and when he finally spoke, it was to say: "I don't like to accept the fact of this occurrence but I guess I'll have to. It's all well and good when you have control of these powers, but when they operate without your knowledge or consent, that's something different. Suppose you walked in your sleep and had somehow gotten over to my house without realizing it, spoken to someone there who had recognized your condition and had brought you back to your apartment, and then awakened you. Upon returning to consciousness and being informed of the trip you had made, you would have to be presented with pretty substantial evidence to believe it, wouldn't you?"

"I certainly would," I agreed.

"But once you had been convinced of what you had done," continued Harry, "wouldn't it have caused you great concern that you might repeat it?"

"I suppose it would," said I.

"Then you can begin to understand how I feel over this happening," said Harry. "I know, in a way, how it came about. After dinner, Mother and Auntie lay down for their afternoon nap and Josie, Ray, and little John went home. I sat down in my big chair and thought I would do a little reading. I got to thinking of you folks and your kindness in sending us the basket of fruit. I reflected that I would be seeing you on Sunday and, being somewhat drowsy, I relaxed and must have dropped off to sleep. How long I slept, I don't know. But I could have been unconscious at the time Mr. Cousins recorded that he had seen me and taken this message from me. However, Mother and Auntie were up from their naps and back in the living room, where I was reading, shortly after two-thirty.

"My interest in you people must have provided the urge for me to leave my body and appear at the Canterbury. I was apparently aware that you weren't in, for Mr. Cousins states that I didn't inquire if you were home, simply leaving a message that I would see you Sunday. This indicates, too, that I had no conscious intention of calling on you that day or I would have asked for you. It is obvious that this faculty operated, on this occasion, without my conscious knowledge and control, and that's why I am so troubled about it."

"You may be," said I, "but I, for one, am glad it happened. It provides a well-witnessed instance of phenomena of a rare type. I would personally appreciate it very much if you would help me get a signed statement from all the members of your family, testifying to the fact that you did not leave the house on Thanksgiving Day. I would also like to get a signed statement from Mr. Cousins recounting his experience. And I wish, Harry, that you would permit me, at some later date, to make use of this case in a way that would be of help and enlightenment to others who might be interested."

Harry did not answer for quite a time. His eyes had a faraway look in them. Finally, his consciousness came back to him and he said: "All right, Harold, I will consent to your request on one condition—that you do not make this visitation public until after I have departed this life. I must not have any notoriety over this. So few humans really understand, and it would only greatly embarrass me and disrupt our household. I'll have to be extremely careful in the future that I keep this kind of manifestation under absolute control."

Harry J. Loose died on November twenty-first, 1943.

Following are the signed statements of the four adults present in his home that Thanksgiving Day, 1941, together with the account of William Cousins, witness to this most unusual phenomenon.

December 20th, 1941

Mr. Harold M. Sherman,
1746 No. Cherokee Ave.,
Hollywood, California.

Dear Mr. Sherman:

A reply to your request can be made clear in one individual letter containing all the information desired and not signed by myself alone but by the four of us who know the circumstances in detail.

I and my husband, Raymond A. Burkhart, with my small son, John, had Thanksgiving dinner with my parents, H. J. Loose and Mrs. Emily H. Loose, who reside at 123 No. Elizabeth Ave., Monterey Park, California, directly across the street from my own home at 122 No. Elizabeth Ave.

The day under mention is that of Thanksgiving Day, Thursday Nov. 20, 1941. On finishing our 12:30 noon dinner, my mother and my aunt, Miss Dorothy Hesse, went to the rear of the house for their everyday after-dinner sleeping period of an hour or less. This was at 1:30 P.M. exactly by the front-room clock. The hour was announced by all of us as it was a little later than the usual lying-down period of my mother.

My husband, Raymond A. Burkhart, and I and my small son John lingered but a few moments, possibly five minutes, at the door and on the front porch, talking to my father, and then we crossed the street to our own home. My father bid us good-by on the front porch.

He was dressed in his old pants but had on a blue dress shirt with a gray and black figured tie. He also had on his old house slippers. His shoes were in the closet off the bedroom where my mother and aunt were sleeping.

My husband, my boy, and myself crossed the street and got out our car from our locked garage and within the next few minutes (guessing—6-8) we left in the car. My father was still in the house, visible through the front window, sitting in the big chair and reading a book. The garage doors at 123 No. Elizabeth Ave., were closed and his car was not out. It could have been no earlier than between 15 and 20 minutes to 2 o'clock when we drove away. The above ends the knowledge of myself and husband as to the whereabouts of my father on this November 20th, 1941, Thanksgiving Day.

The following is the observance of my mother and aunt in continuation. My mother and aunt woke from their nap, one waking first and disturbing the other to wakefulness. They woke a few moments earlier than 2:30 P.M. by the bedroom alarm clock but conversed and did not arise until the half-hour hand pointed to exactly 2:30.

They both came together into the front room and there was my father with his slippers still on and his vest open, still reading a book. The large front-room clock indicated some minutes later than 2:30 P.M. This would not mean anything particular however as there is always a few moments' difference between the two clocks.

From the personal knowledge of us all, four signers of this letter, my father had not left the house on this day and it would have been impossible for him to present himself at your place of residence at the time that you indicate— 2:30 P.M. of this day.

Trusting that the above answers your question fully, we remain,

Sincerely,
*Mrs. R. A. Burkhart, R. A. Burkhart**
*Mrs. Emily H. Loose, Miss Dorothy Hesse**

The Canterbury Apartments
1746 North Cherokee Ave.
Hollywood, California

December 27, 1941.

Mr. Harold M. Sherman,
1746 N. Cherokee Ave.,
Hollywood, Cal.,

Dear Mr. Sherman:

I am writing you, as you suggested, a detailed account of my experience with what I now consider the most thrilling happening of my life.

On Thanksgiving Day, November 20th, 1941, about 2:30 P.M. in the afternoon, while on duty as desk clerk in this apartment house where you live, I was seated at the switchboard talking to a guest in the building, whom I cannot recall at this time.

When a gentleman came up to the desk, I excused myself and asked what he wanted. He was dressed rather unusually for the day and, too, I thought, not the type to be calling on one of our guests.

Under a strain of some kind and with a strange facial expression, he said, "Will you take a message for Mr. Sherman?" I got the pad and waited for the message. Then, after a slight hesitation, he began very slowly and clearly as though it was a very important one.

"Tell—Mr.—Sherman—Mr.—Loose—will—see—him—Sunday."

After each word he made a face as a person would who had false teeth and had difficulty keeping them in place. He then asked: "Have you that correct?" I said I did, and he left.

The guest I had been talking to remarked: "He was a strange one, wasn't he?" I then stood up, thinking he might have heard her remark, and to see if he had rested on the sofa before leaving, as he had seemed out of breath and not natural.

I then noticed that he had left the lobby although I had not heard the front door open and close, as I customarily did, so I felt free to answer her remark. I said, "Yes, he *was* strange. He certainly wanted to be sure his message was delivered." I then went on with my conversation with her after putting the message in Mr. Sherman's box.

Due to the size of our apartment house and the many people I come in contact with, I gave this no further thought but went on with my duties.

Mr. and Mrs. Sherman returned about 3 or 3:15 P.M. and I called to them and gave them the message. Mr. Sherman said, "It's too bad I missed Mr. Loose. I will call him up."

About 3:30 P.M. Mr. Sherman came down to the desk and asked me about the caller, saying he had phoned Mr. Loose, who lived in Monterey Park, some fifteen to twenty miles away, and he said he hadn't left the house. They had a family reunion and a big Thanksgiving dinner and Mr. Loose had been at home all the time.

I thought this very strange, and Mr. Sherman asked me to describe the caller. I said he was a man in his fifties—rugged complexion—wearing a cap, brown sweater, and dark blue shirt. He appeared like a working man. Mr. Sherman said that described Mr. Loose perfectly as he had seen him dressed on other occasions, and that there must be something odd about the experience, and he would talk to me later about it.

I then said I thought it odd Mr. Loose didn't ask if Mr. Sherman were at home or for me to call Mr. Sherman—but he had just said he wanted to leave a message for Mr. Sherman. I also explained the facial expressions and hesitation in his speech.

Mr. Sherman thought that odd and said he hadn't noticed that about Mr. Loose—but that my description was his all right, as he was a man who believed in being natural about the house, and the family were just real regular folks who didn't stand on ceremony as to dress for festive occasions.

A few days later, Mr. Sherman visited Mr. Loose in his home and discussed the experience of Thanksgiving Day with him, and Mr. Loose became very concerned and wanted to meet me and hear the experience from me.

He came in the side door of the apartment house, wearing the same clothes he had been wearing Thanksgiving Day, except for a lighter shirt. I stood up and said, "Good morning, Mr. Loose," and he asked for Mr. Sherman. I said I didn't think Mr. Sherman was in, and at that time Mr. Sherman stepped up behind Mr. Loose, when he found I had recognized him.

I became a little excited and said, "This is the gentleman who called on you Thanksgiving Day." They both laughed and Mr. Sherman introduced Mr. Loose to me, who explained that the darker blue shirt he had worn on Thanksgiving Day was now in the wash.

Mr. Loose then asked me to explain what had happened on Thanksgiving Day and I repeated to him what I have related above.

Sincerely,
*William A. Cousins**

* These original signed statements together with Mr. Cousins' memorandum slip and the note received by mail from Mr. Loose are in my files. I also have a photograph of Mr. Loose as he was dressed that day.

5. THE NATURE OF YOUR SOUL

HAVING HAD EVIDENCE that the soul of man can manifest itself, on occasion, through its spirit body while man yet lives on earth, it is now possible by means of observation, personal experience, and accurate deduction to determine much about the true nature of this soul.

It is at once clear that your soul dwells not only in your physical body but in your spiritual form as well. You can never see your soul but you can feel it and sense its presence as the very essence of that consciousness which says, "I am I," to you. Without your soul you would have no individual consciousness, no awareness of being, no form, no existence. Your soul is the real you and because of it you have identity, individuality, personality, essential intelligence, and ego.

No scientist has yet been able to define or explain consciousness. Why an inner voice should quietly but persistently, positively, and continually say, "I am I," to you is a great and unsolved mystery, the answer to which is known only, at this stage of your development, by God, the Great Intelligence.

The physical form which your soul occupies while on earth is not you. You are only destined to have the use of this body instrument for a comparatively few short years. Then, however healthy you may be now, you can be certain that either accident or the deterioration of old age will eventually so impair your body that you will no longer be able to reside in it. It is then that this "I am I" of you will take its departure in the spirit body which, up until death, has remained invisibly and magnetically attached to your physical form.

If you need any further proof that your physical body is not you or any part of you but is only the instrument through which you manifest, consider the possible loss of an arm or leg and various organs of this body. Has this loss altered or taken away from your identity or consciousness in the slightest? Your answer, of course, is "No." Even great sections of a man's brain can now be removed by surgeons with no impairment of his mentality. There is naturally a limit to the body's endurance and when it has become too badly injured or diseased, your entity or soul can no longer function through it.

If a posthypnotic suggestion is given to a subject under control, he will feel no pain in a certain area of his body. He can be returned to consciousness and a needle or knife thrust into this area without his experiencing any feeling. Sensation, then, is essentially a faculty of consciousness and not a physical quality, else no suggestion would cause a subject to be insensitive to pain.

In man's normal state of consciousness, his intelligence permeates the body and he is instantly aware of discomfort or pain occurring in any portion thereof, even to the extent of a slight pebble in a shoe. Without intelligence there can be no awareness and the moment your intelligence or soul leaves the body at death, your form has nothing remaining to animate it. It is like a disconnected radio with no operator to activate its mechanism.

You can see from this illustration that your body does not possess your soul. If it did, your soul, as a part of your physical form, would have to die with the body. But, instead, your soul possesses your body and is thus able to discard it, as an outer garment, at death.

The soul part of you is not limited by a consciousness of time and space. It is existent in the forever-now. For it, there is truly no beginning and no end. But your concious mind is limited in its concepts by the five physical senses which testify only to what you see, hear, taste, touch, and smell. It tries to tell you that you had no existence in any form before you were born into this life and that you will pass out of existence again with the death of your physical body. But this conviction, based upon surface observations only, is at complete variance with the testimony being offered by the consciousness of your real self or soul which says, "I am I," and never admits to a time when you were not or a time when you will not be.

Stop this instant and listen to the voice of your own soul. What is it saying to you?

Endlessly, continuously, and positively, "I am I," the same statement of immortality over and over again, the eternal assurance of your *being* as an evolving part of God, the Great Intelligence.

"The Song of Life" from the *Bhagavad-Gita* gives this inspired interpretation of "I am I":

> Never the Spirit was born
> The Spirit shall cease to be never;
> Never was Time it was not,
> End and Beginning are dreams.
>
> Birthless and deathless and changeless
> Remaineth the Spirit forever,
> Death hath not changed it at all,
> Dead though the house of it seems.

This is the state of your soul. It is axiomatic that something cannot come from nothing. There could never have been a time, therefore, when you or any other human creature were totally nonexistent. You must have existed in some form, not yet conceivable to you, or you couldn't be here today. As infinitesimal as you may consider yourself in the great creative scheme of things, you have, nevertheless, been included in that scheme by the Creator of this vast universe.

You are in no position, in this pinpoint of time, to judge the possibly great and unimagined end result of your individual soul's evolution. Could you see ahead in time, untold millions of years hence, you might then encounter this same soul you now possess, so highly developed by the tremendous experiences it has undergone as to have attained a knowing fellowship with God, the Father of all things. Do not then make the mistake of belittling your soul's capacities and the importance of your life as applied to the duties and responsibilities of this world in the opportunities for development now before you.

You were cared for, protected, and brought into conscious being from the most remote reaches of the timeless past to play your part now in the drama of life on this earth. Do you doubt that this care and protection and creative provision will be any less in the boundless eternity ahead?

Before you came into being, no one on earth could have predicted your arrival. And you would *not* have arrived but for an unbroken succession of causes and effects extending back into incomprehensible time. If there had been *one* break in this creative line, *one* mishap along the way, you would not have appeared at the moment you did. But why your particular identity appeared then and not centuries ago or was not destined to appear in centuries yet to come and on *this* earth rather than some *other* inhabited planet is one of the mysteries of this great creative power we call God.

You must accept the fact of your existence here as occurring in accordance with a creative design and pattern of so colossal a nature as to be inconceivable to us who see only the surface of a carpet of life woven by unseen intelligent forces. But you have proof that you represent a *unique value* in the universe because your personality and individuality is unlike that of any other human who has ever lived or will live. The great creative power is not producing any exact duplicates. Each human soul is distinctive and different, as though created with the free will and opportunity to occupy a special place no other soul is designed to occupy in all eternity.

Your soul, because it is a part of God, the Great Intelligence, has access to great intelligence itself, but you cannot interpret knowledge unless it comes to you in the form of experience. For this reason, your soul may possess ageless wisdom which will remain unavailable and unrecognizable to you until you reach sufficient spiritual development to comprehend and utilize it.

In every generation there are individuals who have reached such development, combining the knowledge acquired through experience with the higher wisdom possessed by their soul. This wisdom usually comes to consciousness in moments of meditation or concentration, appearing as an intuitive flash. These flashes often bring new ideas into the world, new inventions and new inspiration of such worth and power as to elevate their possessors to positions of leadership in their respective fields.

Man, at large, has permitted his soul to slumber. He has drugged himself with the illusions of his five physical senses. He has depended only upon information he has secured from without, much of which is false and inaccurate. He has accepted the education of his time which has given him an accumulation of supposed facts upon which to base his often misguided judgment. Not knowing how his own mind really operates and not believing it possible consciously to contact his own soul and derive higher knowledge from it, man lives his life almost completely insulated from the core of his own being.

He is like the iceberg with seven-eights of himself submerged. His conscious mind is the one-eighth above the surface of life, trying to function in the mistaken belief that it represents the whole. Occasionally, during an intense emotional experience, the disturbance reaches beneath the surface and causes the conscious mind, in its gropings, to realize its own inadequacy and the necessity for reliance upon that greater intelligence contained in the subconscious.

Your soul is actually the seat of all that you really are. You can communicate with it through right thinking. It contains your entire intelligence, both bestowed and acquired—your complete memory of every meaningful thought and action in this life, plus an enlarged capacity for feeling and sensing far beyond the five physical senses.

Unfortunately, the limitations of language compel the use of words which in no way adequately describe the functions of the soul. It possesses the power to adapt itself to all manner of conditions and circumstances you may encounter, both here and hereafter. This means that it has to have God-given resources, unlimited in extent, to call into being as your need arises. If you are closely attuned to your soul in this life, the answer to your needs will be promptly supplied. Those who are not so attuned will suffer much for lack of the wisdom and creative force which the soul conveys under proper direction.

Creative power exists in all planes of being—physical, mental and spiritual. Through the function of your sex organs, you are enabled to perform an act of creation on the physical plane and thus, in miniature, participate in an experience common to the great Creator of all things. You cannot, of course, create life, but you can provide new physical forms after your own kind in which life may manifest and new souls become resident therein.

On the mental plane you may also create, giving birth, through the wisdom gained by experience, to new ideas, new and better ways of doing things, and new talents. On the spiritual plane, creation takes the form of newly developed traits of character, new understanding, and new power of expression, all of which add up to soul growth. In all of these three planes in which you live, move, and have your being, you are calling upon the same great God-given creative power within, which is a property of the soul, manifesting itself as required on these different levels.

No man knows of what a thought consists. Science cannot analyze a thought or dissect it in the laboratory or view it through a microscope. Yet the force of one thought can change the entire course of civilization. There can be no consciousness, however, without thought, and consciousness is a fundamental attribute of the soul.

Thought will one day be found to possess structure and substance of such a refined, magnetic quality as to be beyond the registration of our present sensitized instruments. Science has already established, through the electro-encephalograph, that the brain gives off waves which fluctuate in accordance with the nature of the thoughts and emotional reactions in the individual. But it should be pointed out that these are *physical brain waves* and not *thought* waves. All that science is recording is the *effect* of thought action upon the brain instrument, through which thought manifests itself.

The brain is an electro-chemical machine. It does not contain thought or create thought. It simply *responds* to thought. Its sensitized mechanism delivers this thought in terms of impulses over the entire nerve network of the physical body so that the thought is *felt* by the complete being at one and the same time.

Perhaps this concept may be best illustrated by describing the action of a self-service elevator. This intricate mechanism for operating this elevator is its "brain." Beside each elevator door is a push button connected with wires through which electrical current courses each time a button is pressed. The mechanism, however perfect, cannot function until and unless an initial *outside* impulse is given it. But once this impulse is received, the mechanism goes into action and faithfully reproduces specifically what is required of it by the nature of the impulse.

In much the same way your intelligence, resident in the soul, acts upon its instrument, the brain, giving it orders in the form of strong desires and feelings. These become currents of energy, activating certain cellular structures and sections of the brain. The brain then translates these "entitized" impulses into ideas, words, and actions familiar to your conscious mind in its contact with the external world in which you are now living.

The true language of the soul is expressed in *feeling,* not in words. Your soul never speaks to you in words, always through *feeling.* It is you who interpret these feelings with words. Even in your sensing of "I am I," you are voicing an all-powerful feeling.

Often you become so lost in the physical feelings communicated by your five physical senses that you permit them to black out or color the higher feeling emanating from your soul. At such times you deny yourself the wisdom of your accumulated experience, held in store by your soul to be passed on to you as needed.

You should realize that you are evolving your soul by the nature of your thoughts and acts upon this earth. You can weight it down and retard your own development and progress through failure or refusal to follow its dictates as presented to you in the form of intuitional flashes and strong, positive feelings having to do with questions and decisions constantly rising in your consciousness as you face the various experiences of life.

Your soul, as a gift from God, the Great Intelligence, can grow and become a conscious part of you only as you develop and learn to utilize the spiritual powers it possesses. You can *save* your soul from your own degradation only by lifting yourself in thought and act to the high level of possible attainment it holds for you.

Remember, as a creature of free will and free choice, you are never compelled to take the upward path of soul development. It is therefore possible for you ultimately to destroy yourself and your own individual soul by choosing the path which leads to eventual disintegration of your personality and individuality as you conform in thought and act to the destructive rather than constructive principle in nature.

It is important, then, that you do not make the mistake of thinking you have no responsibility to bear in the matter of attaining life after death. You have a very definite responsibility. It is required of you that you earn the right to participate on the higher planes of being provided by God, the Great Intelligence, for all His creatures who elect of their free will and choice to continue the upward climb in His ever-expanding and ever more glorious creation.

You have been given all of the elements and intelligence needed as tools to build for yourself a permanent spiritual abode in the eternal house of God, your Father. To the degree that you apply yourself in an effort to gain lasting soul values from life experience, you will find that the spiritual laws of the universe will be in harmony with your efforts and add their power to your attainments. To the degree that you reject the promptings of your soul and neglect to seek anything of lasting value through life experiences, you will be depriving yourself of the aid of these spiritual laws and seriously impairing your possibilities of survival on the higher planes of being.

Immortality must be earned. God has given you life and a soul to do with as you will.

What is your choice?

6. REINCARNATION—FACT OR FANCY?

REINCARNATION has been one of the great questions of all times, and one of mankind's earliest beliefs. Man felt it to be a satisfactory explanation for life's seemingly unjust tragedies. He could not blame God when kind and deserving human creatures were born blind, deformed, mentally retarded or crippled. He must look to himself for the reason.

He observed that since there was a cause behind every effect, it would follow that he must eventually pay a penalty for harming another human being. But since the cause was not always apparent in his present life, he reasoned that it must lie in a previous life. Thus, if he had willfully blinded someone, he would—some day in some other life —experience a similar affliction.

It seemed to him not only just, but understandable, to attribute every unhappy physical and mental condition to a forgotten misdeed in a previous life. He could then accept whatever handicaps he possessed as a specific form of punishment.

This belief is accepted by millions in countries like India. Born into certain caste systems in abject squalor and poverty, Indians have made no effort to rise above it. They have been taught to believe that this is their karmic penalty and that they must submit to it if they would hope to expiate their sins of the flesh.

The phenomenon of hypnotic regression has revived interest in reincarnation virtually overnight. Through this system of hypnotic control, a mesmerized subject is suggestively taken back in time. He or she is then caused to relate names, dates, places and experiences which are purported to have been a part of a past life that this person has lived on earth. These aspects of hypnotic regression are very dramatic and can well impress the inexperienced, unqualified or unanalytical observer.

Many wishful thinkers and strong believers in reincarnation have declared such demonstrations, however fragmentary or lacking in substantiation, to be proof positive that we have lived before on this earth—or some other—and will live again.

But let us consider what actually happens under hypnosis. First of all, it is now widely recognized that every hypnotized subject has one dominant, all-impelling desire: to please the hypnotist. He wants to say what the hypnotist wants him to say, and he will call up every faculty of memory and past experience and association and imagination to enable him to do so. In addition, he will draw telepathically from the subconscious mind of the hypnotist, with which he is in sensitized attunement, since his mind is under the will control of his mesmerizer.

A startling smattering of information may therefore emerge from the subconscious of the hypnotized subject, even words and sentences in foreign languages with which the subject is entirely unfamiliar in his conscious state. But this still does not establish reincarnation as a fact. It demonstrates only that mind possesses an amazing ability to create, as best it can, whatever is desired of it or by it.

Actually, if an individual were really regressed to the subconscious memory of a previous existence in a foreign land, he or she would speak only that tongue and would exist only in the consciousness of that time. He could not be in *that* time and still be conscious of existence in *this* time. He would express himself as he had expressed himself then, totally devoid of the capacity to draw upon the memory, the experiences and the language of the personality that he represents in this present life.

This point has not been stressed in the examination of hypnotically regressed cases, in all of which subjects have imitated only an Irish brogue or English accent or Germanic tongue, and mentioned foreign words or phrases, seldom launching exclusively into a foreign language. This would indicate that the subject is not dealing with past experiences that happened to him but has fabricated certain incidents as an author would gather material about a character for a story.

When a person is regressed to a time in his *present* life when he was very young and asked to print or write his name, he may reproduce it almost exactly as he did then, and speak as he then spoke, indicating that the subconscious, like the grooves in a phonograph record, does possess an exact recording of what has taken place, at all times. If, then, we have lived before, somewhere in our deep subconscious there is just as exact a record of all past lives.

Could we tap such a record, we could immediately have access to a comprehensive knowledge of other languages, the ability to speak and think in these languages, as well as a recollection of all past experiences.

Some believers in reincarnation contend that we are motivated by the essence of past lives without the ability to recall any specific information pertaining to these lives. But you cannot have an essence unless you can have contact with the substance from which the essence is extracted. Your present consciousness either is in touch with the memory of a past experience or it is not.

Some say that you must attain a certain degree of soul development before your past lives are revealed to you, implying that there is some kind of a spiritual over-control.

This is in direct contradiction to those who maintain that a psychically endowed individual can, through autohypnosis, recount the highlights of your past lives. Anyone with any fair knowledge of past historical periods could conjure up names and incidents in his imagination and identify them with personalities living today. There could be no possible way of proving the truth of such so-called "revelations" which the either gullible or wishful-thinking individual must accept on faith.

At one "reincarnation party," where the guests assembled were costumed to represent the character in history they had been told they formerly were, *four* Cleopatras appeared! The clairvoyant had apparently encountered a shortage of prominent women in history and had caused Cleopatra to be reincarnated in four women at the same time! He had never bargained, of course, that their respective paths would cross in this life!

It is satisfying to many men and women who have been living a humdrum or frustrated life, to feel that they have been a "somebody" in a past incarnation. This serves to compensate for the fact that they have accomplished little or nothing which they consider worthwhile in this existence. Perhaps this is why the idea of reincarnation has such an appeal. It is an alluring form of escapism.

It is my conviction, expressed in other chapters of this book, that we have lived before, that we have always existed in some form, if only as an idea in the comprehensible mind of God, the Great Creator. But it does not follow that we can recall this prior existence during a session of hypnotic regression.

It is obvious that our physical bodies have evolved from what we term "lower states of being." In the eyes of our Creator, such states are perhaps not lower states at all, but simply states of creative progression on the path toward an ever-increasing self-conscious awareness of our existence in the vast world within and without ourselves.

It is conceivable to me that we, as human creatures, have come up through countless gradations of life until we have arrived at an embodiment in this wonderful electro-chemical organism which enables the intelligence that we possess, and have developed through indescribable past experience, to manifest itself in this plane of being.

It is possible that this is what advanced souls have called a "first life planet," and that the human intelligence having evolved to this stage is finding its first expression as a self-conscious creature, aware of its "I am I" identity. Such a creature would have vague and fragmentary feelings of having lived before in some state but would be unable to specifically trace these past experiences, since this would be the first time it would be individually conscious of what was happening to it as an entity. He has gained this self-conscious awareness as a result of an evolutionary status above all other known animals on this earth. He can, as a consequence, look toward a future of unlimited horizons!

Everything that man can possibly conceive, he can one day possibly achieve. There, it is evident, is where the way divides. Here is where man reaches up to grasp the hand of the unfathomable God who made him, and seeks to make self-conscious use of the God-given powers he finds within and about him. Here man senses, perhaps for the first time, that he is actually a transient, occupying a physical body for a limited period on this earth to gain the experience and wisdom necessary for his next and continuing evolutionary adventure.

He has discovered that everything he has needed for his development on this planet has been provided by an Intelligence of limitless capacity, and he has faith that this same Intelligence has provided everything he will need in successive planes of existence as he moves on in time and space!

If this be the scheme of life, why is reincarnation necessary? Why, instead, may not birth and death, and birth again, be simply progressive evolutionary advances from one life form to another, wherein we carry over certain specific characteristics which we call "personality," as well as a basic identity which is never lost as long as we choose to progress?

Isn't it conceivable that there are planes of being, ad infinitum, that we carry over from one plane to another only what we have developed from past life experience, but that, having now reached the stage of self-conscious awareness, we will remember, from this earth life on not only *who* we are—but the essential experiences that have happened to us as creatures of comparative free will?

We know that the human embryo gives evidence that we have emerged on the physical side of life from body forms which, at one time, possessed gills and even a tail. The fact that these body forms have changed and refined themselves into the sensitized instrument we now inhabit indicates that an evolution of the soul is taking place concurrently with the evolution of the body.

Your intelligence, having arrived at this state of development, has demanded and created the marvelous instrument through which you manifest yourself; and the next body form you will occupy has already been created for you as a higher vibrating counterpart of this one, and will be ready for your use when you vacate the physical house in which you are now residing.

There has not been, nor will there ever be, any break in your evolutionary spiral so long as you retain the urge to go forward, to learn more about yourself and your relationship to God. This urge is implanted in human consciousness on its Godward side. Even the lowliest of men at times sense the beckoning call of the Infinite—the ever-present invitation to strive for individual betterment—to lift themselves from the mire of their own making and find a better way of life.

More and more, as we come into an understanding of the deep purpose of life, we realize that life is basically an individual proposition. It is up to us, at all times, as to how we use it and what we do with it. It is a great and mysterious gift.

I believe that we exist beyond life but can only manifest ourselves through life—that the soul possesses the body. This is an important distinction to emphasize because, did the body possess the soul, it would imply that the soul must die with the body. But the spirit is independent of the physical form which it permeates and animates. Our existence in any one body form is transitory, but our existence apart from all body forms is as permanent and lasting and imperishable as the existence of God. We must be a vital, even though infinitesimal part of God, the Great Intelligence, or we could have no existence at all.

I can perceive how certain highly developed souls, desiring to return on missions of service, might employ higher creative laws and cause themselves to be reborn in new earth bodies. It would require high development for such accomplishment and would not mean that the human race, as a whole, was a part of such a plan or could so return. The suggestion has been made that Jesus was such a reincarnation—Elijah returned.

Where cases have been reported of entities returning who have recalled past lives, it is my opinion, as a result of my lifelong investigation of such phenomena, that this constitutes what is called "obsession." There have been a number of such cases, reported and investigated by scientists, wherein two distinct personalities have resided concurrently in the same body, each expressing different characteristics as well as separate memories.

When you consider that the intelligence is not the body, though it expresses through the body, you can understand how, under certain conditions, a discarnate entity might find a way to take temporary residence in a body belonging to another person already on earth.

Ordinarily, each of us is insulated against such intrusion, as a radio set is protected against two broadcasting stations coming in on the same wave length. But there are rare occasions when this insulation is broken down by emotional disturbances, or by too deep a delving into the unknown, which makes the mind over-receptive to outside influences. Under such circumstances, what is called obsession may occur. This is not a split personality experience; we are speaking of two separate, distinct personalities.

There have been occasions where the invading entity has demanded to be taken to the home of his or her parents in a different part of town or even in a different city, demonstrating an accurate memory of a past existence as a son or daughter, calling loved ones by name, recognizing them by sight, and showing a complete familiarity with surroundings, past happenings, and friends.

This could not be classified as a reincarnative experience since the indwelling entity did not belong in the body, and had simply found a way of expression through it. At intervals the original possessor of this body would return and express himself or herself as completely unfamiliar with surroundings and people, asking to be taken back to his or her home and parents.

Nevertheless, such experiences serve to prove that we do exist beyond so-called death, that we are merely temporary tenants of our earth bodies, that we possess higher vibrating bodies in a higher vibrating plane of existence. Under so-called normal conditions we do not return here or need to return. When an obsession exists, it is obvious that the rights of the original entity have been usurped.

No one knows at what moment following conception the intelligence that is you identifies itself with the body form which is then created.

But it is conceivable that advanced souls who may return to serve mankind, arrange in some electromagnetic manner beyond our comprehension to indwell a new physical body. Such an arrangement would not, in these instances, deprive another intelligence of its opportunity to experience an earth life, since no intelligence save that of the advanced soul would enter this body in the first place.

This is simply conjecture at this point. There is no proof, as such, that advanced souls have come to earth in this manner. But, from what we are now beginning to learn about mind and matter and the domination of matter by mind, we can so theorize.

7. THE VALUE OF LIFE EXPERIENCE

ONCE YOU ARE LAUNCHED upon what has often been called the sea of life, it is up to you to swim or sink.

From the very moment you are born, you must draw the first breath in order to live. If you are slow in so doing, the doctor will aid you by a slap on the rump or such other measures as may be required to produce this first breath, and start your body functioning.

You cannot continue to live without effort. You must not only breathe to live but you must eat to live. And while your memory of these first few infant years on earth is buried deep in your subconscious, you were nevertheless growing and developing physically and mentally as you reacted with your quickening five physical senses to the conditions around you.

Experience, the great teacher, has been by your side since your first baby cry announced the arrival of a new soul on this earth. Whatever you are today you owe to the way you have reacted to everything that has happened to you.

How have you faced sorrow, tragedy, disappointment, domination, defeat, discouragement, criticism, frustration, economic insecurity, disillusionment, ill health, and a host of other soul-testing occurrences in life? How have you responded to joy, encouragement, success, praise, achievement, wealth, freedom of expression, good health, and all the other so-called good things of life? What have these varied experiences brought out in you as an individual?

Are you the possessor of strong fears, hates, prejudices, jealousies, selfish and lustful desires, uncontrolled emotions, severe repressions, resentments, inferiorities, despondencies, and a wide variety of destructive emotional character traits? Or have you, instead, acquired, for the most part, such attributes as the courage to face all conditions in life, a love of humanity, a freedom from prejudice against any religion or race, emotional stability, self-control, an aspiration for higher attainment, a happiness in doing for others, a true understanding of your own self, and a satisfying philosophy of life?

Somewhere between these extremes of human experience and development, you and your soul are today situated.

It is quite possible that you have not realized the fundamental spiritual purpose behind life experience. You may have viewed the things that have happened to you as having little value beyond the moment in which they have occurred. There have no doubt been many experiences you would have avoided if you could and quite a number so unpleasant or even tragic that you would like never more to remember them. But everything that has happened to you—either for good or bad—has brought a change in you for better or for worse.

It is now becoming more and more apparent that each soul brings into his life a pattern or design of living which has been prepared for the individual's guidance on earth. There is no question on the physical plane but that, at the moment of conception, the exact blueprint of the body a specific soul is to occupy comes into being. A mysterious, directing creative intelligence takes charge immediately and sees to it that each of the untold millions of multiplying cells plays the exact part designated in the perfect formation of the soul's earthly instrument.

In much the same manner, but on the mental plane, a blueprint comes into existence specifying the potentiality of each individual soul. No two souls possess exactly the same potentiality any more than two personalities, even twins, are precisely alike in appearance, temperament, character, and expression.

The soul seems to have possessed, at the moment of birth, a sensing of the future possibilities of the new entity. It holds the mirror of these possibilities up to the inner mind of this individual in the form of definite urges and desires along certain lines and in certain directions. The individual may or may not be aware of his soul's promptings as he faces various life experiences and arrives at turning-point decisions. Too often all contact is lost with the soul, and the entity, depending only upon the testimony of his five physical senses and such knowledge as he has gained without, fails to live up to the potentiality within him. Sometimes circumstances are too overpowering for a weak-willed individual to change, even though he may feel himself to be in the wrong profession and position in life.

You often hear the statement made that he or she "has found their right niche" or "they have discovered what they were best fitted for" or "he or she was just born for that job." These fortunate individuals either developed such an understanding of themselves as to have known intuitively what they were best equipped to accomplish, or they have lived in such harmony with their inner nature as to have responded instinctively, under guidance of their soul.

Much of the discord and unhappiness of life has come about through humans who have not lived up to the best that was within them due to their failure to recognize or utilize potential talents and abilities they could have successfully developed.

Are you among them? Are you occupying the place in life that you feel you should be? Have you sought and created the right opportunities for your own development along the lines of your choice? Are you doing what you have wanted most to do and what you feel, inwardly, you can do best? If you feel you have failed somewhere along the road of life, can you determine where and why?

It isn't failure that need count so much. It's the *way* you have reacted to it and the value which you should have extracted from it. Only through the testing of experience can you come to know your own strengths and weaknesses. There is no substitute for the attainment of this knowledge.

Memory has been given to man as a soul attribute, so that he may learn to profit by his experiences. His ability to recall a mistake he has made in the face of a life situation enables him, if he has developed sufficient resolution, to correct this mistake. Without memory he would be totally incapable of overcoming his weaknesses or bettering himself in any way.

The lowest animals have little or no memory. Their reactions are largely instinctive. Their potentiality for development is therefore limited, whereas man, of all creatures on earth, through the higher faculty of memory has no limit placed upon his mental and spiritual growth. This alone is evidence that man is destined for continuing life and experience beyond his brief existence here.

You may have rebelled over the many little and seemingly insignificant things you have had to do over and over, the routine things of life, which you feel have taken up your time to no good purpose. But it is often these supposed little things, whether they be of a personal, domestic, business, social, or spiritual nature, which might ordinarily prove annoying and which you can eventually rise above, that help perfect your quality of character and ability to achieve big things in life.

Big things, in themselves, are only a multiplication in intensified form of a myriad of accomplished little things. Everything you have ever mastered in life remains to serve you. Everything you have *not* mastered remains to hamper you.

How you look upon what you are required to do is most important. You may have felt that your tasks in life are so routine and menial as to be ashamed of them. You have an inner craving for recognition and appreciation which your present occupation or activity cannot bring you. The world, unhappily, does not have a high respect for certain extremely necessary professions such as street-cleaning or ditch-digging. Yet without them our modern civilization would be impossible. Again, it is the wrong sense of values and not the jobs which should be held in contempt.

Given the right perspective, you can be completely happy serving your fellow man and God by performing a task which may be regarded as insignificant in the eyes of those who still do not realize how dependent each human is upon the services of others. All of the elements in and about you are intended for your service, once you have learned to attune your mind to them and command their servitude. Every desire which you picture in your mind starts the creative power within you working to materialize this desire in your outer life. There are actually mysterious and wonderful magnetic forces in your consciousness which, once activated by your desires, commence to attract the conditions, circumstances, and people which you need to bring to your life what you have pictured.

You may not have realized this to be true, but this creative power has been functioning either for or against your best interests in direct accordance with the nature of your own desires from the moment that, as a child, you first became conscious of your being. In this manner, every other human who has ever lived, now lives, or will live has exercised, is exercising, or will exercise this great creative power.

Because the desires of humanity at large have been so filled with feelings of hate, lust, greed, prejudice, resentment, and revenge, they have visualized unhappy pictures and produced unhappy results throughout all recorded time. Such conditions will continue to be created by mankind, despite all attempts at peaceful world governments and prevention of world wars, until humans change their thinking, because the creative power of thought is more potent than governments and armies and atomic bombs.

You can see, as you gain an understanding of the universal laws behind your own *being,* that you are actually creating the world in which you live. The world, therefore, *cannot* change until *you* change!

There are religious-minded people, however, who mistakenly believe that since humans are born in sin and are captives of Satan, it will require an act of God to save them. This attitude, as has been emphasized before, has discouraged many humans from putting forth the effort to overcome their weaknesses or to combat the conditions of evil existing on this planet. But those who have gained a true understanding of the universal laws know that God, the Great Intelligence, has left man to his own devices here, as elsewhere, to work out his destiny through experience, under guidance of that higher intelligence resident in his own soul, if he so chooses to call upon it.

The expression of love in all its phases of human relationship is the greatest developer of the soul. The highest concept we can have of God is love. The religions of the world exhorts us to love God in return for the love and mercy which God bestows upon His own creation. Man has attempted, throughout the ages, to express this love through various forms of worship but, because man has often misinterpreted his relationship to God, he has feared rather than loved this Great Universal Being.

To bring the God of creation down to the level of man's understanding and experience, it has been necessary in the past to personalize Him. Unthinking humans could not comprehend an Intelligence so stupendous that it could exist as a part of individual consciousness and also permeate every portion of creation throughout the boundless reaches of time and space. Yet the advances of science make it clear that such a concept of God is not only rational but the only acceptable and logical one in the light of present-day knowledge.

With our finite minds, so limited by the five physical senses, we are incapable of picturing the actual form which a vast Intelligence would occupy if, indeed, the God of creation exists in form, as we conceive of it, at all. It is enough for us to know, and to be able to prove, that the Godforce and intelligence which has given us life, and the opportunity to develop a soul possessing survival value at death, should actually dwell in our consciousness.

The greatest experience which can come to us in this

life is, therefore, to discover our true relationship to God. This discovery cannot be made *for* us; it must be made *by* us.

How wretched and alone many individuals are who lack this assurance of God's presence in moments of great trial, tribulation, suffering, despair, and crisis! How serene and self-assured, with heads unbowed and dauntless spirit, are those who have come to know that a higher, finer, something dwells within, and that however trying the life experience, their attunement to this greater power can and will see them through.

What is your present attitude toward life? Are you consciously building for the future in terms of improved soul qualities or are you devoting most of your thought and energy to securing and maintaining things outside yourself which can have no lasting value but into which you have poured your life hopes and aspirations?

Perhaps never before, in all recorded history, has man's life on earth been made to seem more fleeting and insecure. A few atomic bombs can destroy his civilization, his home, place of business, himself, and those near him. Even a prolonged drought can dry up a water supply and withhold moisture, so that a great state like California and a community of some millions, such as the Los Angeles area, can be severely crippled. These threats to man's security and physical existence, only two of many, merely emphasize the transitory nature of his life here and the fact that the earth was not intended as a permanent abode of his evolving soul.

No two humans, however, possess the same individual destiny nor react similarly to the same experiences. Your geographical location and the race into which you were born are great determining factors, but it is possible to arrive at the same degree of soul development whether you be a native of India, of Russia, of France, Germany, Italy, Great Britain, Japan, China, Ethiopia, Brazil, United States, or any other country.

What you think and feel as you undergo experience is having an immediate and constant effect upon your soul. It is tragically true that millions of humans in the world today, beset with hunger, starvation, poverty, economic and political unrest, and privation of every sort, are living or existing under conditions hardly conducive to real Soul growth. Many of these distressed and tortured humans are so filled with hate, resentment, fear, despair, sickness, loathing, and the weary struggle simply to live from day to day that little light reaches through to their under-nourished souls.

This is the great crime against mankind, this denial, through man's inhumanity to man, of each individual's free-born birthright—the opportunity to develop his own soul.

Even so, through exercise of will and faith and dogged perseverance against all manner of human sufferings, disappointment, and dire subjection, there are men in every race, in every country, and in every form of unhappy environment who are rising above all conditions and obstacles and achieving great soul development. That these are the exception rather than the rule demonstrates nonetheless that man, in his deep inner self, possesses a something more than animal and that this something, once reached and clung to and permitted to express itself through man, can lead him to victory over all opposing elements in this sordid material world. Where many seemingly fail in this life struggle, the few who eminently succeed hold the torch of human faith and hope high, that those who follow after may take new courage to continue the fight as best they can with the inner equipment at their disposal.

It serves no purpose or value to attempt to present a fanciful, happy, Pollyannish picture of life on this earth. The past centuries reek with the tortured, anguished screams of untold millions whose blood and lives have been needlessly spent through wars and persecutions, all a result of man's greed, intolerance, and insatiable lust for power.

Despite the attempted beneficent influence of various great religions, the very separateness of these religions has brought about divided human feeling so fanatical and so intensified that countless millions have been killed and are being killed today in their name. Can you possibly conceive of any just and almighty God condoning such slaughter by His own creatures in support of their faith in Him, whatever that faith may be?

These are questions you must face, and logically and impersonally answer in the presence of your own soul, if you are to free your mind of false concepts and become a real force for good in the world of humans who must recapture a sense of spiritual values or destroy themselves.

Your soul, being the one imperishable part of you, possesses the only lasting value. Once you have anchored yourself to your soul in consciousness, you can see the foundations of the world being shaken and still retain the confident inner assurance that you, yourself, are standing upon firm spiritual ground. Millions have, today, lost this inner assurance. Cut off from their real inner selves, they have denied themselves the guidance and wisdom otherwise possible to them and which they must have if they are to gain ascendency over their animal passions which are now running riot.

God, the Great Intelligence, never commands His free-will creatures to obey His universal laws; He only invites them. Man is constantly punishing himself by willful disobedience of these laws. There is no wrath of God expressed in these punishments. The laws of the universe operate impersonally and automatically. Go counter to them and you suffer the consequences in accordance with the degree of your opposition. Attune yourself to them and you gain the benefit of their power in like accordance.

It is difficult, when whole masses of people have lost their contact with the spiritual force within them, to see any evidence that they possess a higher and finer something. It is there, nevertheless, awaiting release, proper nourishment, and expression.

Given economic relief and freedom from hunger and want, the millions now suffering throughout the world would soon recover their spiritual grasp and emerge from their terrible experience with added qualities of soul. It is not the easy life, in most instances, which contributes essentially to soul growth. Those who have undergone the most severe mental, physical, and spiritual trials are often afforded the greatest opportunity for reaching the highest inner development if they have had the fortitude to meet life experiences to the best of their ability.

Look back over your own life. Have you learned more from your successes or your failures? Largely through wrong have you learned the right. Through trial and error you have discovered new and better ways of doing things. Reading and study may have helped, but the testing of your knowledge in actual *doing* has been required before you could make what you learned a real, active, and useful part of you.

In childhood, you first had to become acquainted with your physical body and how to use it. As a baby almost every move had to be trained and developed. You were taught to employ your hands and arms in reaching for things by shiny objects suspended before you. The act of walking had to be mastered step by step, after many falls. It was not a simple matter to learn how to eat properly at the table, nor to speak. You have long since forgotten those early struggles which probably still remain in the vivid memory of your parents, but you were gaining, even then, experience necessary to your increasing life expression and the ultimate achievement of individual independence—the ability to think and act on your own.

Experience has been waiting for you at every turn on the road of life. To take a deep breath now is a new experience, to have a thought, to make a move in any direction, to see or hear or feel anything of even passing interest. Something is happening every second in your body and in your consciousness. As long as you have life you must react emotionally to whatever occurs without and within you. Your reactions are bringing about changes in thought and character and soul quality, either for your good or ill, dependent upon the nature of such reactions.

How you get along with others in your own family and neighborhood is largely determined by what you have built up in yourself. If you are self-centered and self-seeking, your attitude will make it difficult for you to enjoy happy and understanding human relations with others. Unable to analyze your own faults, you may resent this failure to win their approval and develop hatreds and prejudices. Such a reaction is a defensive mechanism, helping you to gloss over your own hurt but not to correct your deficiency.

If you are to benefit from life experience, you must develop the daily habit of self-analysis and honest self-appraisement in order that you may see yourself, at all times, as others see you. Be ready, then, to discover your own faults and weaknesses, taking steps to eliminate them before they are called to your attention or become so much a part of you as to attract unhappy conditions and results.

Try to keep in mind at all times that an equal part of God, the Great Intelligence, dwells within every other human, as it does within you, regardless of race, color, or creed. He may not be demonstrating this God-power in his life expression at the moment, but it is there within him, nevertheless, ready to respond when awakened and developed.

Rather than criticizing your fellow men because of their difference in thought and act, you should strive to remember your kinship with them through this eternal relationship you all bear to God, the Father. No one person can be any less "a child of God" than another. We are all on different rungs of the ladder of self-development, and some of us, through right reaction to life experience, have become more advanced spiritually than others. But the opportunity exists for even the lowliest to climb this same ladder if he will. God's hand is there to help him up, through this higher intelligence within him, once he reaches for it.

Do not make the mistake, then, of considering yourself a more favored son of God because of your greater enlightenment and supposed superior position in life. The higher and finer your development, the greater responsibility you should bear to those less fortunate.

You cannot compel another to think your way or discover evidence of God's presence in his consciousness as you have discovered it in yours. But you can, through your fellowship and understanding, touch the heart and soul of another and cause him or her to realize that you possess something much to be desired which they, in turn, may be inspired to seek within themselves.

Look, then, for that fineness within each human which is actually there even though, perhaps, not yet expressed. When you are ill-treated by another, school yourself not to react in kind but to inquire, if you have not merited such abuse, what has caused this individual to act as he has. It is quite likely that if you put yourself in this person's place, with his developed temperament and under pressure of his experiences in life, you would be sharing his very thoughts and feelings. Considered from this viewpoint, you will be able to exercise a far greater tolerance in your relation to others, and the very fact that you return good for evil by not showing resentment at their mistreatment will do more to disarm and actually to punish them in conscience than any attempt to repay them on the level of their own conduct.

You will need to protect yourself, of course, at times from those who would maliciously take advantage of you economically, physically, mentally, and even spiritually. But you gain nothing by permitting yourself to develop and hold feelings of hate, resentment, prejudice, and disgust toward others.

Learn to demagnetize yourself from the conditions such individuals bring with them. Wherever possible, endeavor to dissipate or destroy these conditions through appealing to this finer something now deeply buried in their own undeveloped souls. One never knows when a chance word, expressed at the right psychological moment, or an unexpected kindly deed, or a sincere demonstration of interest in a thwarted, rebellious, inhibited, or misguided personality, may penetrate a calloused outer shell and bring about a response from within sufficiently strong to provide a turning point for the better in this person's life.

It has often been said, "There is some good in even the worst of us." It is much more effective to appeal to that good in others and to draw it out than to recognize the bad and emphasize it. Tell a child that he is bad and you make him more conscious of the mistakes he has committed. Recognize evil in another and this individual will not be inspired to show you his good side. It is only the most depraved who will not respond and try to live up to the estimate you place upon them.

Every human soul, however high or low in self-development, craves appreciation. They must have it from someone whom they respect in order to preserve their self-esteem. Without self-esteem there can be no self-development, for the urge to improve one's condition in life is then lacking.

The greatest deterrent today to mankind's individual development and progress is the division in thought, felt and expressed by humans of different races and creeds and colors. Humanity, like a great chain, is actually as strong as its weakest links. These weakest links, if not strengthened by humanity as a whole, will eventually break and drag all civilization down.

Religion is not reforming the world. The stark truth must be faced that religion today has separated itself into armed camps, either for or against some other sect or cult, and the battle to the death is on to preserve one faith over another. You must be aware of what is taking place on this planet whether or not you are in the midst of this religious contention, for it is, nevertheless, in many subtle ways impinging upon your life experience in terms of each day's routine activities of business or household, rounded out at night by a social occasion with friends or at the theater, repeated with variations day after day. But intangible things are happening to each individual at the same time which are having an effect upon his consciousness above and beyond his week-in and week-out pattern of life. He is being reached through a barrage of magazines, newspapers and books, radio and television programs, motion pictures, and the like, all of which are presenting pro and con thoughts and ideas in dynamic, appealing form.

Unless he has trained himself to think and evaluate, he may be influenced by some thoughts and ideas which can prove damaging to his way of life. He is affected, too, by the economic stresses and strains of the time and the political confusion and conflicting ideologies between countries which are now existing.

He observes wanton evidence of graft in high places in government, business, labor, and military circles, and he asks himself, "What price honesty?" wondering privately, on occasion, how much it really pays to maintain high integrity and honor in a world where many are living off the fruits of others, by their wits rather than their developed skills or work.

These conditions are in the very atmosphere round and about each human in the world today, causing him to wonder and to doubt and to ask inevitably if the God in whom he has been taught to believe really can exist. The churches report and view with alarm a widespread growth of paganism. Yet man's loss of faith in a personal God has come about largely through loss of faith in himself and in the institutions and governments man has erected for his own protection and development.

Because of this lack of faith, this disunity in man's thinking, small, highly organized minority groups, believing fanatically in a way of life, can move in on great incoherent masses of population and take them over, even though such small groups may be unprincipled and their theories of government destructive in nature.

You, as an individual, feel helpless in the face of such forces as you observe to be functioning in the emotionally distraught world of today. There seems to be nothing you can do to help avert what appears to be a coming cataclysm. Yet any change in humanity as a whole can only come about as the result of a change in the consciousness of humanity itself.

We cannot wait on religion, as such, to change the world. And, since governments only supposedly reflect the will of the people, we cannot expect either governments or churches, made up of humans, to save mankind until and unless the humans themselves, through right thinking, bring about their own salvation.

You are familiar, however, with the old spiritual statement: "If God be for me, who can be against me?" You can, through reliance upon this higher intelligence within your own soul, protect yourself and your soul from whatever may happen to you in this world without.

This is the only protection which many men, thrown into concentration and slave labor camps, subjected to every conceivable kind of bestiality and torture, have had against man's fiendish inhumanity to man. Certainly they have found little of value or of joy in this life and, if religiously inclined, must have tormented their souls with the agonized question: "If a God exists, how can He permit such mistreatment of His children by His own fellow creatures?"

Were this life on earth, so tragic and terrible to many, the only life experience, then those humans, apparently innocent victims of certain unfortunate geographical locations, have been most unjustly treated and would, if given individual choice, knowing what they would have to endure, choose not to have been born at all. Yet even their sufferings will have had their compensation if a continuing life of the soul brings a reward in higher states of existence which might justify the price they have been called upon to pay.

Life is usually dear to every human who rebels against the thought of annihilation and oblivion, and clings to this existence with a tenacity which defies starvation and torture, however severe. If God were a personal God in the sense that many believe, with the power to step in and supersede His own universal laws, and if such a God possessed the compassion, love, and mercy attributed to Him, He would long since have prevented man's inhumanity to man. Any loving father would not stand idly by and permit one son to kill another, nor would a God who bore the same personal relation in a creative sense.

But while God, the Great Intelligence, can become a *personal experience* in your life and mine, we can realize that His attitude must, of necessity and in all justice, be *impersonal* as it concerns humanity and His creation as a whole. It has been said that "the rain falls on the just and the unjust alike."

It is important to repeat that, given life and the opportunity of developing a soul, we have been left by God to work out our own individual destiny through exercise of free will and free choice. God has not deserted us in this world of strife and bloodshed. *We* have deserted Him. He is here in us, beside us, and around us, in all nature and in all things, ready to serve us just to the degree that we learn to call upon Him and utilize the unlimited creative and spiritual power which is ever-present.

You should accept, then, whatever experiences come to you, the good and the bad, the happy and tragic, with the resolution to extract a constructive value from them. Many humans have come to regard what they once considered the worst failures and calamities of their lives as their greatest blessings in disguise. Without these happenings, they would not have felt compelled to develop certain strengths of body, mind, and spirit necessary to surmount the circumstances, conditions, and obstacles they had to face. The history of mankind is replete with the record of countless thousands who have been crushed by experiences upon which others have risen to new and finer heights.

It is absolutely essential, if you would get the most and the finest out of life, that you learn to conquer fear in all its aspects. Fear is the great destroyer of faith, hope, ambition, courage, resolution, persistence, and inspiration. Fear has defeated many men and women who have possessed the character and the ability to accomplish much.

Fear of what others may think, fear of criticism, fear of competition, fear of comparison, fear of loneliness, fear of facing the truth, fear of change, fear of making decisions, fear of assuming responsibility, fear of incompetence, fear of uncertainty, fear of the future, fear of disease, fear of physical suffering, fear of old age, fear of death, and countless other fears have ruined the lives of millions in every age.

Free yourself from fear by the realization that "God is not in any one place but *everywhere*." You are not alone in your battle of life. You have a power greater than all the odds against you, constantly by your side. Knowing this in your own mind and heart, even death will lose its

terror and no failure or tragic circumstance can defeat or
demoralize your spirit within.

Conscious now that you possess a soul in process of development through life experience, let that soul speak to
you with the God-given wisdom it contains as a guide in
your every thought and act. Let it speak to you through
the inspired words of Fra Giovanni:

I am your friend and my love for you goes deep. There
is nothing I can give you which you have not got, but
there is much, very much, that—while I cannot give it—
you can take.

No heaven can come to us unless our hearts find rest
in today. *Take Heaven!*

No peace lies in the future which is not hidden in this
present little instant. *Take Peace!*

The gloom of the world is but a shadow. Behind it,
yet within our reach, is Joy. There is radiance and glory
in the darkness, could we but see—and to *See* we have
only to *Look*. I beseech you to *Look*.

Life is so generous a giver, but we, judging its gifts by
their covering, cast them away as ugly or heavy or hard.
Remove the covering and you will find beneath it a living
splendour, woven of love, by wisdom, with power. *Welcome
it,* grasp it, and you touch the *Angel's hand* that brings it
to you.

In everything we call a trial, a sorrow, or a duty, believe
me, that *Angel's hand* is there; the gift is there, and the
wonder of an overshadowing *Presence.*

Our joys too; be not content with them as Joys. They, too,
conceal diviner gifts.

Life is so full of *Meaning* and *Purpose,* so full of *Beauty*
—beneath its covering—that you will find earth but cloaks
your heaven. *Courage* then to claim it; that is all! But
courage you have; and the knowledge that we are *pilgrims
together,* wending, through *unknown country, home. . . .*

8. ARE YOU WORTHY OF SURVIVAL?

IF YOU WERE GOD and had created a race of human creatures with free will and free choice and opportunity to develop as they chose, would you require anything of them in return for this gift of life and promise of a soul? Would you let each individual creature continue to participate with you in this vast scheme of creation, in the ever-expanding universe of countless worlds and states of being, if some of your creatures showed no appreciation of life and no inclination to better themselves in any way, either here or hereafter?

As an earthly father or mother, would you not finally feel compelled to disown a wayward child who, even in adulthood, after having been given every chance for right thinking and conduct, persistently disregarded or rejected every chance for self-development and self-advancement? Would not such a human eventually disown himself insofar as anything you might be able to do for him might be concerned?

You well know that it is a human impossibility really to help others until they are ready and willing to help themselves. You cannot live the life of another for him no matter how much you may sympathize with or desire to bear his burdens. If you protect or shield an individual from facing a life experience, you have not done him a kindness. You have only weakened him. If you have encouraged your children to lean upon you, you have, to a considerable degree, destroyed their self-reliance.

If it was God's intention, as is indicated by man's nature and position on this earth, to let man evolve his own soul in accordance with his own desires, then man must assume responsibility for his own conduct and not throw himself upon God's mercy when he goes wrong.

Religion has done man a great disservice by telling him that he has been born in sin. It has placed an unholy stigma on the functioning of sex and the laws of creation. The person who is pictured as possessing the greatest spirituality is he or she who has remained a virgin and has kept himself or herself untainted by sex experience. Most of the great spiritual leaders are men who have never married and who are not recorded as having consorted with women.

The implication is clear that those who stoop to sex experience, even with the sanction of the Church in lawful marriage, can never attain to the spiritual heights of a man or woman who denies these natural urges.

How damning and inconsistent is this point of view when you consider that without the sex act, as provided by God and nature, man himself could not exist or continue his species. Had the sex act itself been unclean, it is unthinkable that God would have provided this function in the first place.

When sex has been debased, man himself, through wrong exercise of free will and free choice, has debased it. But each child born into this world must be pure and innocent in the sight of God, whether or not it is judged by man to be legitimate or illegitimate, since the child had no choice or accountability in the matter and came into being as the result of the functioning of God's creative law.

It is a tragedy, of course, in our modern civilization, if a child is born outside of wedlock because such a one is damned by society for life. Yet all life must be sacred to the Creator, regardless of the interpretation man places upon it, and some of the world's finest men and women of all ages have been termed "illegitimate." Had their origin not become known, society would have accepted them wholeheartedly with pride in their accomplishments. In most instances, however, these persons have had to win their place in the world against great resistance and no little condemnation.

Something is fundamentally wrong with man's concepts of life and of God when he starts with the religious premise that the creative act which brings him into being is evil, and that the highest spirituality is to be attained by those who refrain from the sex act completely. This concept defeats, at the outset, the desire of most men and women to reach spiritual heights in self-development. Having surrendered to their normal sex urges in expression of their love for one another, through marriage, these husbands and wives may live virtuous lives but feel themselves to be forever inferior in spirituality to those who, through supposed higher religious scruples, have remained single.

Upon what standards is true spirituality to be judged? In the orthodox Christian world much stress has been laid upon Christ's birth through the Immaculate Conception of the Virgin Mary. We are told that God set aside the normal laws of His creation and stepped in as the Holy Ghost to impregnate Mary, wife of Joseph, and cause His only begotten Son to be born of woman but not of man. This suggests that no pure and undefiled creature could be created as the offspring of the mating of man and woman.

Christ, then, on this basis, came into the world as the incarnation of God, in human form, possessing a spiritual power from the moment of birth far exceeding that ever possessed by any ordinary human in all world history. This being true, what credit does He deserve for having lived "the perfect life" when He did not exist as an ordinary man but had the power of God in Him, capable of resisting evil and overcoming all temptations common to man?

How much more credit would He have merited had he been born of man as well as woman and had He attained the true "Sonship with God" through spiritual development and had then met and mastered the forces of evil by calling upon the God-given powers within His own devel-

oped soul? What hope and inspiration and call for faith in
Him and His spiritual achievements would such a life have
held for all humanity!

As it is, however, Christ's promise that "there shall be
those who shall do greater works than I," can be only hol-
low mockery since it should be obvious that no humans in
any age have possessed or could possess the spiritual
power of the "Son of God" and could therefore never attain to His spiritual level or accomplish greater works than
He, regardless of the effort put forth.

But consider how transcendent and inspiring this same
promise of Christ that "there shall be those who will do
greater works" would be if we had accepted Him as a man
among men who had attained to the stature of a God
through elevating His own consciousness in spiritual
thought and earthly living. We could then believe wholeheartedly, through inspiration of His perfect life example,
in the actual possibility of our duplicating His experience
on earth and even exceeding it in accordance with His
promise.

Instead, however, Christ's spiritual accomplishments
are placed upon an unobtainable pedestal. We are taught
to look up to Him from a position far beneath Him in spirituality and are discouraged from the thought or desire of
becoming like Him. Our nearest approach to Christ can
only come by throwing ourselves upon His mercy, asking
forgiveness of our sins, thus purifying our souls and attaining salvation, not through self-development but only
through faith in Him.

By this procedure, we are herein given the concept that
God, after creating us as "imperfect human beings," has
taken and *is* taking a sadistic joy in seeing us wallow in sin
and then grovel at His feet, begging mercy and forgiveness.
Where is the dignity and majesty of man under such conditions? But far more pertinent, where is the dignity and
majesty of *God?*

It is regrettable that those who founded religions felt it
necessary to set their spiritual leaders apart from the rest
of mankind, attributing to them spiritual powers to which
no one else could attain. It is tragically unfortunate that

the wonderful creative principle contained in the functioning of sex should have been so desecrated by religion that the finest expression of love which man and woman can know on this earth has been surrounded by the odium of sin. To think that such a taint is placed even upon the birth of a child that it must be baptized and blessed by a representative of God in order that its soul may be safely brought "within the fold" and its salvation assured!

Can you conceive of the God of this universe receiving or rejecting souls of His newborn creation on the basis of such narrow-minded, man-made technicalities? Yet there are many believing humans who are horrified at the thought that some of their relatives or friends have not been baptized and are therefore not candidates for survival.

Religion should welcome constructive criticism without the fear that religion will be destroyed by it. Faith should not fear investigation—else how strong is faith?

When I attest to my firm conviction that man survives death and can attain an immortality of soul, I am stating a basic tenet of most religions. When I further state, as pertains to the Christian religion, that I believe in the spiritual principles extolled by Christ, the truth of which can be demonstrated in actual everyday living, I am also in fundamental agreement with the teachings of the Church.

Is it incompatible, then, for me to declare that I can get far greater help and inspiration from the example of Christ's life by accepting Him as a human being, like myself, who found the way of life and the only approach to God through a self-conscious and self-inspired development of his own soul?

I can have faith in such a concept. I can believe, then, that we are *all* "Sons of God" in the making. I can have respect for Christ and His great spiritual accomplishment and still retain respect for myself, freed of the stigma inherent in the religious concept that I was born in sin. I can see God in all of my fellow men and women and realize that, as we strive to follow the pattern of thought and daily living set for us by a man among men who mastered and demonstrated these universal spiritual laws, we, too, can approach His understanding and accomplishments and, one day, as we gain in brotherhood of all races, can even surpass the great works of the Master.

In keeping with the scientific progress of today, which gives every indication of eventually bringing about a harmonious union between science and faith, the *form* of religion must change. Christ devoted His life to attacking the *unyielding form* of the church of His day. Christ Himself did not found a religion. Religions were founded on Christ's teachings and about Him after His death, and these religions have become as set in form and tradition as those which Christ fought when alive.

All forms in nature change in the normal evolutionary process and the form of ritual and ceremony and creed of all religions can and must change to fit the new and ever-expanding mold of man's spiritual and scientific knowledge, if it expects to survive and be of vital service to man.

Christ, two thousand years ago, clearly set forth the unending clash between the old and the new and warned that *new form* must be created to contain the *new*. His parable is worthy of repetition here:

> . . . no man putteth a piece of new garment upon an old; if otherwise, then both the new maketh a rent, and the piece that was taken out of the new agreeth not with the old.
>
> And no man putteth new wine into old bottles; else the new wine will burst the bottles, and be spilled, and the bottles will perish.
>
> But new wine must be put into *new* bottles; and both are preserved.
>
> No man also having drunk old wine straight-way desireth new; for he saith, "The old is better."
>
> (Luke 5-36:39 inclusive)

Man, a creature of habit, tends to cling to the old and, being familiar with the old, as Christ has stated, often considers it better. The whole onward march of civilization against the resistance of outmoded forms and systems of thought testifies to this unhappy fact.

In our day we can still reach back to the now antiquated horse and buggy as a form of conveyance. Our elders can recall the first advent of the horseless carriage and the predictions, freely made, that no human being could stand a speed of twenty miles an hour. As the automobile gradually won popular favor through its perfection, it brought great cultural changes in its wake—new roads, new means of rapid communication and transportation, new forms of social intercourse, new means of education by travel and consolidation of schools, new unification of peoples, the opening up of new frontiers, the establishment of new communities and manufacturing, mining, and farming sites, new ways of thinking, and new moral codes. The introduction of the automobile into the life of the world marked an entirely new era in transportation and had a tremendous impact upon the consciousness of mankind.

In a similar and no less tremendous way, radio, television and the airplane have annihilated time and space and changed the thoughts and habits of the peoples of earth. They have awakened mankind to the exciting realization that our concepts are not limited to one world; that countless other planets, inhabited by intelligent beings may exist; that there are invisible worlds and realities beyond the reach of our five physical senses; and that man's knowledge of himself and the universe about him is only just beginning!

These ideas required *new forms* in which to be expressed. Such ideas would never have come into existence in a horse and buggy day, without the forms these ideas demanded.

Religion today is in danger of destroying its spiritual function and usefulness by holding to a form of creed as outmoded as the belief that the earth was flat. Once religion has had the courage to scrap these forms and to unite in a common brotherhood on the basic belief in one God, Father of all, and placing responsibility for salvation upon the individual's self-development, there will then be released such a flood of spiritual truth as to bring about changes in man's mental and spiritual being commensurate with the great changes which have come to man through the stimulus provided by the new forms of automobile, radio, and airplane.

Man will then know that he contains within himself qualities which, once developed, are worthy of survival. Today, millions are fettered and held in spiritual bondage by old, outmoded forms of religion. They are still singing that "the old-time religion is good enough for me," but do they comprehend upon what this old-time religion has been founded?

Do they know, for instance, how the present-day books of the Holy Bible, considered the inspired Word of God, came originally to be chosen? Every spiritually-minded person in this age should be acquainted with this knowledge in order to evaluate properly the contents of the Bible in his search for truth.

The books that made up the Old Testament came from manuscripts originally written by different Jewish and Egyptian authors. Each book contains the name of its narrator except Genesis, Kings, Chronicles, Jonah, and a part of the Psalms. These manuscripts were first written on soft bark or soft impressible stones, and many more manuscripts were written than have been preserved. This is true also of the manuscripts comprising the New Testament, which were produced and preserved in a similar manner, and all of them were collected about three hundred years after Christ lived.

By the year 325 A.D., a vast number of writings had been gathered together, including about fifty gospels or books relating to Christ and the apostles, along with other historical and sacred records. Because of their conflicting nature and diverse points of view, their existence was the cause of much dissension among the spiritual leaders of those times.

Accordingly, at the command of Constantine, two thousand and forty-eight bishops were assembled at Nice to debate, discuss, and select, by common agreement, those books from among this assortment of manuscripts which, in their judgment, constituted the "authoritative Word of God."

It must be remembered that these bishops were ordinary, uninspired human beings, who possessed strong personal convictions and prejudices and beliefs in certain peculiar doctrines, and each of them was desirous of seeing to it that his own predetermined concepts should prevail.

So vociferous were they in declaiming their beliefs and preferences and so violently argumentative did these proceedings become that Constantine was finally compelled to step in as an arbiter and to disqualify seventeen hundred and thirty bishops from having a voice in deciding which books were and which were not the "Word of God." This left remaining only three hundred and eighteen, all of whom were generally in agreement with the preconceived ideas of the Emperor Constantine.

Sabinus, the bishop of Heraclea, in describing these men, has said that, "excepting Constantine, himself, and Eusebius Pamphilius, they were a set of illiterate, simple creatures that understood nothing." As an evidence of how lacking in mentality this group of early bishops was, Pappus recounts that "having promiscuously put all the books that were referred to the council for determination under the communion table in the church, they besought the Lord that the *inspired* writings might get upon the table, while the spurious ones remained underneath." Legend has it that, "This happened accordingly."

No intelligent human today, however, will accept such a story as fact. But we have sufficient record of the nature of this conclave of bishops and the mandatory action of Constantine to know how the books of our present-day Bible were chosen. We are consequently led to wonder if many of the books then destroyed might not have contained more elements of truth.

Out of some fifty gospels then existent, it was decided by these bishops that those only of Matthew, Mark, Luke, and John were worthy of being preserved. They rejected entirely the books of James, Jude, and the Apocalypse. With this decision arrived at, Constantine then arose and solemnly declared that the same should be considered as sanctioned by the Divine Will, and that the books, as selected, should thereafter be implicitly believed as the

Word of God. He then ordered the rejected manuscripts to be committed to the flames.

In the case of the writings of Arius, Constantine issued an edict decreeing that all his works should be burned and that any person concealing any writing composed by him, and not immediately producing it and consigning it to the flames, should be punished with death.

Since Constantine held such power to impose his will, all bishops, however intelligent, lived in dread of being branded as heretics, of being calumniated, reviled, hated, anathematized, excommunicated, imprisoned, banished, fined, beggared, or starved if they refused to submit. Under and over such conditions the Holy Spirit is supposed to have presided!

It was not until the year 633 A.D. that the books of James, Jude, and the Revelations of St. John were received into the canon at the Council of Toledo. There had been frequent councils, prior to this time, in which previous decisions were annulled and new propositions established, all of which produced modifications in the *form* of the Bible as well as in the number of books that were to be considered as composing it. But at the Council of Toledo, the Old and New Testaments were established in nearly the same form in which they exist at the present day.

This does not mean that the Bible, so formed, was widely read at that time, for it was not until the fourteenth century that the first English version was made. In fact, had it not been for the development of the art of printing in the fourteenth and fifteenth centuries, it is probable that the Bible would have sunk into oblivion.

Printing, however, enabled priests of the Roman Catholic Church, who had held these accredited manuscripts in their personal possession, to circulate copies of the Bible and thus establish its doctrines, announcing themselves as having the authority so to do. There followed in later centuries, the reformation of Luther and Calvin and serious divisions of Biblical interpretation which have resulted in the various Protestant denominations of today. But this is sufficient religious history to indicate to you the origin of the contents of the Holy Bible and to permit you to judge how spiritually inspired, if at all, its original composition was.

Mankind has been taught to venerate the Bible, on the grounds of its sacred, authentic antiquity and the pronouncement that it consists of the Word of God which can be found in no other book or place. In this connection, it is important to remember that all books of the Bible represent the writings of men who have recorded their impressions and convictions from memory or hearsay of events which occurred long before their actual recording. The accuracy of these accounts is therefore open to question.

Man's memory is demonstrably faulty. His recollection of events of even a year ago, let alone fifty, is not to be depended upon. Christ's disciples were unlettered men. Their accounts were largely transcribed for them after Christ's death. They obviously kept no written records of their experiences with Him, and their testimony of happenings, common to them all, can be expected to have been colored by their differences in viewpoints and observations.

Since Christ himself left no written records, those who wrote the later books of the Bible, depending entirely upon word-of-mouth accounts passed on from generation to generation, were even further removed from the truth and accuracy of what really happened. And when you add to this the method used for selecting and pronouncing these books the inspired Word of God, you can see upon what a precarious foundation this spiritual knowledge rests.

But these facts, largely unknown by the rank and file of church members, do not destroy true religion or basic faith. The great and undeniable proof that the spiritual principles of which Christ spoke really exist can be demonstrated in the life of every human who will put these principles to the test in his own personal experience.

Why, then, should the church attempt to keep mankind in ignorance of its history? Might it not far better frankly confess how its early spiritual concepts and historical records came into existence? Having done this, should it not then place emphasis where it belongs—upon man's opportunity to evolve an immortal soul through developing the God-given creative and spiritual powers contained within his own being?

Such forward steps taken by the Christian religion would open the way for harmonious union with all other religions and create a *new form* through which the long imprisoned spirit of truth could then be manifest.

Today, the discovery of ancient parchments in caves beside the Dead Sea by a shepherd boy have thrown new light upon the origin of the Bible. Known as the "Dead Sea Scrolls," these early records, believed to have been written and secreted by a sect who called themselves the Essenes, 150 B.C., are being carefully deciphered and studied by world scholars.

There is no doubt but that many of our present concepts of Biblical history as well as Biblical truths will be altered and augmented by these findings. Whatever the interpretation of the records contained in these remarkable parchments, the truth and the power of Christian principles to remake the lives of men cannot be changed or lessened.

If this discovery leads to an elimination of certain set dogmas and creeds—discarding the letter and elevating the spirit of religion—the peoples of the world will greatly benefit. The past has a contribution to make to the future, but no man can look backward and forward at the same time. The only hope for humanity lies in the future. For this reason, it is imperative that the minds and souls of all races must be free of false and limited concepts if they would realize this hope of higher spiritual development, individual happiness, and true peace on earth.

Much has been said and written about the great role religion must play in this new atomic age which demands the harmonious union of all peoples, in all countries, for, this failing, we are left facing the sure promise of complete annihilation. There is an increasing clamor arising among farsighted spiritual leaders on behalf of the unification and consolidation of Protestant churches, but this is meeting with widespread resistance as members of various sects cling tenaciously to their particular creeds with a world falling about them for lack of the spiritual enlightenment which could regenerate and revitalize mankind.

In small and large communities, churches, which profess the same basic faith but different forms of worship are struggling for existence, each fighting to gain new and desirable residents as members of their congregations. These churches are not competing for the saving of the souls of these new prospects, their main interest being economic rather than spiritual—a saving of the church's budget.

There are many instances of husband and wife having a divided allegiance, one attending a Baptist church, for instance, and the other a Methodist, with the children also divided, all because each wishes to remain loyal to his or her faith and the individual churches are reluctant to surrender their membership.

You can see, from this prevailing condition, that little emphasis is being placed in the churches today upon development of one's soul and preparing oneself through individual self-conscious effort for enjoyment of the better life on earth and a better-equipped consciousness for the life beyond.

It has been necessary to review the attitude and position of religion, both past and present, so that you might be given a true perspective from which to ask yourself the question which heads this chapter: *"Are you worthy of survival?"*

Such a soul-searching query cannot be answered from the standpoint of religion alone. It reaches far beyond man-made concepts of God and different ways of salvation. You have to be freed of such concepts in order to join your reason with your faith and to judge the value of your own real self and the relation you bear or can bear to your fellow man as well as your God.

You must expand your mind and your comprehension to consider the fact that great civilizations of human creatures, long since extinct, quite possibly once existed on this planet. Where are the souls of those individuals in this present day? From the standpoint of science, if survival is a fact now, it was a fact then—and perhaps other spiritual leaders such as Mohammed, Confucius, Buddha, and Christ evolved also in these long-forgotten races to point the way to God.

If man possesses a soul worthy of survival, it should then be obvious that it is not because of the religion to which he belongs but because of what he has fundamentally become in his interior spiritual nature.

Much, however, as you might desire, personally, to survive death, you should ask yourself if you can logically see or sense any sound reason why it would be of value to the universe for your life to continue. Has it counted for anything worthwhile, as yet, on earth? Has some other human —or humans—been helped or inspired or cheered or made better through your having lived? Have you developed any qualities or abilities or values in this life which you feel you could vastly improve upon with great benefit to yourself and others if granted a greater allotment of time and opportunity than permitted here on earth? Are you earnestly desirous of gaining a better understanding of your own real self and an increasing awareness of and attunement with the God-power within you?

These are all evidences of an awakened soul and the fact that you have positively identified your ego with the spiritual urge toward self-betterment which leads inexorably, in accordance with spiritual laws, to evolvement of soul and the increasing assurance of self-conscious, active, intelligent existence after death.

As you look about you, discerning many people who have no seeming interest in self-development or a possible life beyond, and who are expressing themselves largely on the animal plane of existence, you may rightfully inquire what conceivable end might be served either God or nature by their survival. Many are contributing and have contributed next to nothing of constructive value within themselves to carry into any rational hereafter. They are a burden on those about them, if not upon the state and federal government; they possess scant appeal in their personalities and may even be loathsome to look upon and to associate with. It is difficult for you to fathom how even an all-merciful God could love and respect such creatures.

They may be so wretched that no church would be interested in seeking their membership or saving their souls.

Yet you realize that if you are a child of God, they also are children of God. If you cannot conceive of the possibility of immortality for them, you can hardly grant the possibility of immortality for yourself, for each human soul must be of equal value in the sight of God, its Creator, who possesses a foreknowledge of the unthinkably great potentiality of that soul in the eternality of time.

It is God's point of view, not man's, that we need to cultivate.

A human architect does not design a structure aimlessly and without purpose. Nor is it conceivable that the Great Architect of this universe would have designed and created these countless heavenly bodies of suns, moons, and planets, and all the myriad forms of life thereon, without having some grand eternal plan in mind, in which His evolving creatures may increasingly participate as they earn the right through continued experience and by the acquirement of greater intelligence and spiritual power.

If God, the Great Intelligence, has a plan—and reason and faith both tell you that such a plan exists—then you may be sure that you and every human creature have a part in it. What that part may be, you may not now possess the development or the wisdom or understanding of your inner possibilities to detect, but you should strive from this day on to attune yourself more closely to the God-power within you and thus draw nearer to the time when your evolving soul will reveal to you the job you came here to do and the service you are destined to perform in the great, unending scheme of things.

When this has become your prayer, when it becomes your heartfelt urge, however low in the scale of spiritual development you may consider yourself to be, you have ignited the spark of your divine nature and your worthiness for survival has been established.

9. YOUR LINK WITH THE INFINITE

THE TRUE NATURE of God cannot begin to be grasped by the finite mind of man. We see His handiwork in all nature about us: in all mineral, vegetable, animal, and human life; in the boundless deeps of the restless oceans; on the mightiest peaks of the majestic mountains; in the musical babble of a little brook; in the happy song of the fleeting bird; in the black vaults of starlit sky; in the winds and rains and sun and clouds; in every changing mood and season. In every breath of life we draw, the overshadowing presence of the great creative force is there.

Can it be possible that we—little creature man—are linked with all this? Or are we just one of nature's accidents on the changing sea of life, destined to rise and fall like the crest of a wave and be lost in the sea again? Or have we evolved out of this sea with a purpose which reaches beyond this life on earth and which finds us transformed at death and transported to a new environment where new wonders of God await us?

What could be the nature of a link with the infinite which could assure us of such a destiny? What could lift us above the level of the animal world in which we reside and grant to us the privilege of continuing to participate, as self-conscious beings beyond death, in God's great expanding universe?

What is there in lowly man that might insure his inheritance of such a high estate? How can he look back upon his blood-red past of inhumanity to man and then look forward with spiritual assurance to any merited continuation of his life in other realms?

Why should creature man, throughout all ages, of all animals on earth, have been born with the urge for self-betterment, the desire for a higher, finer life than he has been able to find or make for himself on this planet? What is it that has given to man mind, memory, imagination, and identity? Why has he struggled toward greater enlightenment and greater attainment despite the destructive surges of animal passions within him? How does he rate in the scale of creation in terms of cosmic values?

What is man, anyway, and what, for that matter, is human consciousness?

What is life and from whence does it come? And what is the reason behind it all?

To contemplate these questions of the ages is to experience the sensation that your mind is imprisoned by the bony structure of your cranium. Taught, as he has been, that knowledge is only available to him through impressions received and interpreted from one or more of the five physical senses, man has felt that he did not possess the capacity within himself to comprehend the Infinite or his true relationship to it.

In the outermost physical sense, man, with his limited sensory apparatus, viewing the material world in which he lives, might well have thought himself insulated and cut off from the ability to determine the basic nature of things and the what, who, and why of his existence. Unable to penetrate the mystery of his being, he has sought consolation in the past by telling himself that God hasn't intended him to know these things. Religion has encouraged man to accept this point of view and to rely upon the authority of spiritual leaders and the Word of God as the only explanation possible of man's origin.

But, in all times and in all peoples, there have stirred from the depths of their innermost consciousness, in moments of great emotional crisis or need and in unexpected flashes of indescribable divination and inspiration, impressions which they knew had not come to them through the ordinary physical channels of sense. On occasion, these inspired or bewitched men and women have been worshiped as prophets and saints or vilified and even killed as devils or those possessing evil spirits. But the persistence of these phenomena, so often condemned and feared by the populace as well as religious leaders, indicates, nevertheless, the existence of forms and degrees of intelligence and forces beyond and above the mere physical nature of man.

The seers of ancient times professed the ability to foretell the future through dreams, trance states, mesmeric practices, or methods of concentration. The healers laid claim to the ability to induce the functioning of a healing power by calling upon higher forces acting in and through them by means of special religious ceremonies, incantations, sacrificial offerings, spiritual meditations, and physical excoriations.

In some way, then, not understood but sporadically demonstrated, man was giving evidence of his relationship to and communication with an intelligent force not of his own making and apparently existing, at times, outside his own consciousness. Could man, therefore, be a creature of physical propensities only? Or did he possess, unknown to himself, in his innermost being, undeveloped powers of mind with which he might, someday, through an extension of his present sensory organs, probe the entire universe of time and space?

Steeped in the materialism of the past and often fearing these impressions when they came, unbidden, as evil influences, man resisted his inner urges and even sought to conceal impressions from the knowledge of others that he might not be adjudged possessed or insane. Religion appropriated these phenomena, and where voices were heard and forms were seen and visions were beheld by members of the clergy, priests or nuns, such spiritual manifestations were accredited as coming from God or His appointed messengers. It was sacrilege for a layman to declare that he had been visited by such an illuminating experience.

In the sixteenth century, the Popes were urging the criminal prosecution of witches. Protestantism, zealously interested in protecting the authority of the Bible and its literal interpretation of the Scriptures, also engaged in vicious witch hunts. Humans dared not give utterance to any unusual inner feelings or impressions which came to them, and women particularly feared to incur the ill will of neighbors, well knowing that they might be charged with trying to cast a spell upon them or with being in league with the devil or possessing an evil eye.

By the seventeenth century, the people of Europe had been taught to look for witches, and thousands of innocent humans were rounded up, convicted by the courts, and put to death in Germany and France, and even a few hundred in England. Late in this same century, in the village of Salem, in the state of Massachusetts, in a new country where men and women had gone seeking freedom from religious persecution, an outburst against witches occurred which resulted in nineteen persons being hanged and one "pressed" to death. But, if this were not enough, John Wesley, toward the close of the eighteenth century, declared that "to disbelieve in witchcraft is to disbelieve in the Bible"!

And it is only in most recent times that "psychic phenomena," so called, has been brought out of the wilderness into the scientific arena of parapsychological laboratories. Man is thus slowly but steadily advancing, yet at what an *unspeakable* cost!

There is reason, at last, to look forward with hope and assurance that science will join with Faith in proving not only the existence of man's soul but the continuity of life beyond the grave. Already the higher powers of mind which man has manifested at times, throughout the centuries, have been authenticated by scientific recognition. We still know comparatively little about the nature and operation of these powers, but only time and further experimentation are required to reveal much new light.

Based upon my own personal experience and observations, I would like to make the following predictions:

(1) Man will be found to possess a consciousness which is linked to universal intelligence;

(2) this link will be discovered to exist in and through man's evolving soul;

(3) the brain of man will be proved to be the instrument, only, of his mind and soul, and not the possessor of either;

(4) through higher development of the psyche in man, the true nature of the universe and God and man's own being will ultimately be revealed.

When Christ said: "The Kingdom of Heaven lies within," He spoke a great truth. We can see *evidence* of God's handiwork all about us, but we can never come to *know* God until He has become an inner experience in our own soul.

Man has sought God everywhere else but within his own self. Since he was supposedly born in sin, he could not conceive of any part of God actually dwelling in him. God was a great and distant Being who existed outside of man and whom man must approach through penitence, as a humble, lowly sinner, unworthy to stand in His presence.

Actually, God has been trying to speak to man through man's own soul, sharing with him such inner wisdom and spiritual power as he has developed the capacity to receive. There have been men and women in every age who have found God, in a personal way, on the level of their own acquired higher understanding. They have tried to communicate this discovery to their fellow men in inspired statements and in examples of exalted lives of service, but mankind, as a whole, has remained deaf and blind.

In many instances, those who have sought to reveal the eternal truths, sensed and comprehended by their developed souls, have suffered ridicule, condemnation, and even death at the hands of an uncomprehending multitude. But still, these enlightened individuals have persisted, as though commanded to give courageous voice to their convictions in the face of a scoffing humanity. And down through the ages, these pioneers of thought, like the ceaseless dripping of drops of water, have worn away the mighty stones of ignorance and superstition and persecution until the gleam of truth is, at last, beginning to penetrate into the darkest heart.

How can you get an understanding grasp of your actual relationship to God, the Great Intelligence? It is so difficult to find language which can convey what the inner consciousness, in moments of meditation and inspiration, is able to sense beyond the reach of words.

Had man's spiritual nature kept pace with his material development, he would have brought words into being to describe and define his spiritual experiences. Today, however, as we stand on the threshold of great spiritual discoveries, we are confronted with the poverty of words to communicate the new dimensions of mind which are opening up. Thus such illustrations as may be presented must, of necessity, be crude. Yet some start must be made in an attempt to suggest the nature of man's link with the Infinite.

Consider, then, the telephone system with which you are familiar. You possess an individual phone in your home. Regard this phone as the instrument through which you are manifesting yourself. There is a wire attached to this instrument which connects you with the telephone exchange and you can now, theoretically at least, if all humans have telephones everywhere on this earth, take down your receiver, put in a call, and get any one of the several billions whom you desire on the wire.

Your intelligence is directing this operation, but your communication and extension of this intelligence to a distant point is made possible by the current in wires supplied by a central power station, independent of the instrument you are using and, of course, independent of yourself.

Visualize now this central power station as the God-center of the universe, possessing unlimited energy and intelligence, functioning eternally *on all levels of existence*. Invisible wires or beams of energy are connecting you with all other people and, for that matter, even though not recognized by you because of your present low state of development, with all other intelligence—past, present, and future!

Your capacity for reception is extremely low, so that your perception of the God-power with which you are linked is now exceedingly feeble and limited. But because a part of God, the Great Intelligence, dwells within your consciousness, it provides the link which unites you with the intelligence in all things.

God calls you over this intercommunication system through the medium of your evolving soul, but you must have developed the eyes to see and the ears to hear the higher impulses which are constantly emanating from the central power station, beamed at the *intelligence levels* of all self-conscious creatures, on all planets, throughout all universes, in all space.

Remember, the telephone instrument you are using is not the real you any more than your physical body is the real you. This telephone instrument is an inert piece of mechanism until you activate it by taking down the receiver. The instant you do this a circuit is opened up between you and the operator. You then make known your desire and another circuit is opened, giving you a direct line to the individual you wish to reach. This is all done for you, without any effort on your part beyond placing yourself in a position to receive the message and making the initial connection. But *you* must take the first step or the entire system of communication, with all its power to function at your bidding, will reveal no evidence even of its own existence.

In much the same way, people who have not sought to sense the power of God within their own consciousness have not provided the conditions necessary to contact this power and thus have no personal evidence of its existence. It is there, however, awaiting, with infinite patience, the call of that soul.

But God bears of necessity an impersonal relationship to all His creation. If the current in the telephone wire represents God's power and intelligence, it can only become personal to you when you attune yourself to it and make use of it. The power and intelligence is there for all to use the instant they make a connection. But God is not personally conscious of that part of Him which is utilizing His power and drawing upon His intelligence.

Are you conscious of each individual cell in your body as it derives its existence and undergoes changes and experiences peculiar to itself? Of course not! But the life of your body supplies this cell with all that it needs, unhesitatingly, automatically, and without question, in answer to the demands that the cell makes upon it. This is in accordance with the laws of nature governing your body and the functioning of cell life.

If a single cell had the self-conscious awareness and intelligence to enlarge its concepts, it might eventually grasp, through intensified experience, a more and more accurate knowledge of its surroundings and discover by slow degrees the true nature of your body in which it lives and has its being. But this cell could never, in all eternity, even remotely comprehend your complete nature, for your body is comprised of untold millions of equal parts, each of which would be approaching an experiential knowledge of you differing in character and nature.

It is a basic law of physics that the whole cannot be contained in any of its parts and it should be equally discernible that no part can ever embrace or comprehend the whole. This fact applies also on the mental and spiritual planes of being.

If you can visualize yourself as an ever-living, evolving cell in the immortal God, you can logically see how you will always maintain your relative position while continually enlarging your understanding of Him through experience and soul development, drawing ever closer, in a personal sense, but never achieving absolute perfection since God, alone, is perfect in the functioning of His eternal and infallible spiritual laws.

As this concept of God and your relationship to Him in consciousness becomes fixed in your mind and heart, you will sense a deep and abiding feeling of peace and security. God will no longer seem to be dwelling in some far-off, remote place in the heavens. You will feel His presence within you and your existence in Him. You will know that the real you cannot die even though your body, this instrument you are manifesting yourself through on earth, will one day pass away. You will have the sublime assurance that you are as close to God as any member of His vast creation and that the prayer of a sincere and earnest soul, properly attuned to His God-power, can be answered.

You will come to realize that this God-power within you is creative, and that when rightly called upon, it can and does attract to you the conditions, circumstances, and people you need to help you attain something you have very much desired and have worked to achieve. You will learn that this power, operating *impersonally,* will produce for you wrong results if your thinking and desires are wrong, just as quickly as it will create good results under the stimulus of right thinking.

Thus you must understand that a higher wisdom, granting you free will and free choice, will help carry you to the heights if this is your heartfelt resolution, but will eventually plunge you to the depths if your thinking and desires have taken a destructive turn. You are punished then, automatically, on the basis of cause and effect, the law of compensation dealing out rewards and penalties in exact accordance with the nature and character of your own thoughts and acts. You are, therefore, your own devil, creating you own evil through wrong thinking. This evil, given life and form by your thoughts, will persist as long as wrong thoughts persist. The devastating power of wrong thoughts is being demonstrated today through the mass hatreds, the religious and racial prejudices, the greeds and jealousies, and the savage lust for world domination.

Religionists are praying for God to intervene and bring about a settlement of men's differences before the outbreak of World War III. But God did not step in and prevent World War I or World War II, nor will He stem the tide of man's own making which is sweeping all humanity toward the most horrific and needless calamity of the ages.

Every great invention of man has possessed its good

and its evil side. It is man who has chosen, through reverting to his lower animal nature, to exercise the evil rather than the good. As he has abused the God-power within him, he has punished himself, and this will always be so until man learns to assume an individual responsibility for his own thoughts and acts and realizes that he is actually the cause of all the ills which befall him.

Evil exists because man, as a free will creature, has created it. Evil will cease to exist when man elevates his own thoughts and unites his consciousness with the creative spiritual principles which have the power, at his bidding, to liberate him from the long night of ignorance, superstition, intolerance, and persecution into which his false concepts and wrong thinking have led him.

Once self-consciously linked with the Infinite and sensing himself, as an individual, to be *one* with all humanity, knowing that mistreatment of another human ultimately brings misfortune upon himself, man may be inspired to rise above his animal nature and utilize the God-given powers within him for his own and his fellow man's good.

This is a possibility now lamentably remote, as man's time for learning these great truths grows alarmingly short in the face of his threatened self-destruction. It would be well that man face the terrible consequences of his acts now, for life is so ordered that he cannot escape them in the hereafter.

10. THE AFTER-LIFE

IF THERE IS A LIFE AFTER DEATH, why has it not been possible for man to gain more genuine evidence of it long before this?

The belief in some form of continued existence in a heaven or a nirvana or a happy hunting ground, an in-between world, at astral state, a purgatory, a hell, and even a return to this life, through reincarnation, has persisted among all races of men since earliest recorded time.

It has not been fear of the unknown, alone, which has caused man to invent ideas of a future life. Some vague consciousness has told even the lowliest of men that he is more than mortal. This consciousness comes to him from his higher self, his soul, the one connecting link he has with God, the Great Intelligence, and the vast universe into which he has been born. Because he is still in the kindergarten of life, he has not developed his inner powers of mind sufficiently to know, for a certainty, that he survives death. He has relied, then, upon faith and superstition to fortify him against the unknown and to enable him to face death, when it comes, with more courage and less fear.

Before radio was invented, few people would have believed that the supposedly silent ether could be filled with sounds only awaiting the proper instrument to make them audible. And now, of course, we have the miracle of television which adds sight to sound and means that the image of a man as well as his voice can be projected through space, even around the world, in a flashing second of time. Thus, within our short lifetime, has the power of the *invisible* been revealed to us!

Should we, then, be so ready to doubt the possible existence of other states of being, different enough in vibration to be beyond the reach of our limited five physical senses? A friend might be broadcasting this minute, but if we did not possess the proper receiving instrument and have it dialed to the right wave-length, we would be entirely unaware of this fact. This would not, however, affect the reality of our friend's broadcasting.

Scientists, through extension of the powers of their great telescopes and microscopes, are discovering new universes infinitely large and infinitesimally small. These universes have always existed, but man has only become aware of them as he has developed the means and the mechanism of bringing them within the range of his perceptions. The same will be true of man's eventual extension of knowledge concerning the change called death, what happens when he dies and what state he then finds himself in.

But these secrets of the soul yield only to the person who learns how to commune with his soul. The part of man which does not die, has been trying to tell the physical side of man that death does not end all. But man, relying solely on the testimony of his physical senses, refuses to listen to this inner voice and tells himself that the death of the body ends all. He has observed that all evidence of the life and personality of an individual disappears when his body ceases to function, and because he lacks any developed means of locating the departed intelligence, he concludes that the intelligence has also died with the body.

But a greater wisdom than man's has so creatively arranged the universe that all creatures are required to live one life at a time in one world at a time. Can you imagine how distracting it would be if your mind mechanism were not insulated against the possibility of receiving impressions beamed at it from intelligences in higher dimensions?

Even with telepathy a proved fact, which means that under certain conditions mind can communicate with mind on earth, man's mental processes are such that he has to develop this faculty before it can become operative for him on any actually recognizable and demonstrative basis. It would be most disturbing if your own thoughts could be trespassed upon or interfered with by the thoughts of another without your having any control or means of tuning them out.

Nature accomplishes this tuning for you. It is only rarely that the thoughts of some friend or member of your family, usually in a moment of great emotional crisis, are strong enough to break through the resistance set up in your own consciousness and make you vaguely or vividly aware of something that has happened to him. The fact, however, that thoughts *can* be sent and received, wittingly and unwittingly at times, proves the existence of mental powers *outside* your five physical senses. It suggests, too, that there must be a world of reality in which thoughts travel separate and apart from the world in which you have your physical existence.

Since your body was designed and created only for living on this earth, you cannot expect to find evidence in this body of a life beyond. Your body can only testify that, because it had a beginning, it must and will have an end.

To gain any real dependable knowledge or insight into the possible nature and conditions of life after death, you must turn away from your body and fix your thoughts upon your soul within. It knows that it is destined for higher and finer things. It knows, too, that you possess a spiritual body just as real, in its way, as your physical body now seems to you.

Occasionally, as in some of the cases I have previously described, man catches a glimpse of his spiritual form and hears the actual voice of an entity temporarily removed from the physical body. These often unbidden and unexplainable occurrences have given rise to wide-spread reports of ghosts, apparitions, hallucinations, angels, fairies, and legendary gods. The fact, however, that there has been such a constant reference to these manifestations, with the varied interpretations that have been placed upon them, is proof of the existent phenomena.

There is an old statement that "the exception proves the rule." One absolutely authentic instance of genuine psychic phenomena demonstrates its reality.

When Marconi succeeded in picking up the first feeble radio waves from across the Atlantic with his crude wireless receiving set, he had demonstrated his theory that electrical impulses would not be impeded by the curvature of the earth. From then on, it was only a matter of time until man, employing this knowledge, developed the science of wireless telegraphy, radio, and television as it exists today. In much the same manner, man will eventually discover and utilize the great spiritual powers possessed within himself, but *only through his own self-development*.

Man's intelligence, however, has actually *recreated* in mechanical form the operation of his own mind. In telepathy, consciously performed, man has to use the instrument of mind, and the energy generated by the intensity of his feelings or desires, to send and receive thoughts much after the fashion of radio broadcasting and receiving. Quite often these thoughts, so transmitted, are received by the mind of the sensitive recipient in the form of fleeting but vivid "mental pictures." When this happens, the recipient can be said to be functioning as a "human television instrument."

We have witnessed the tremendous evolution in the form and power of radio receiving apparatus since the first little crystal sets with their clumsy earphones. Oldsters can recall the unparalleled excitement they experienced in trying to pick up the signals from a distant station through the crackling static and their joy when even one intelligible sentence from a human voice or snatch of music could be brought through in an evening's time.

The young people of today accept their marvelous radio reception as commonplace, but there is tragedy in the fact that man has achieved such mechanical perfection and still has shown so little interest in perfecting the powers of his mind. However, his invention of radio and television has forced upon all humans an acceptance of the fact that because a thing cannot be heard or seen is no reason it does not exist. We simply lack the instrument or the facilities for making ourselves aware of its existence.

Intelligence is always limited, to a certain extent, by the form in which it resides. When the early crystal sets outlived their usefulness, the spirit of progress in radio cast them aside and new forms came into being, more sensitized in nature, possessing greater and finer receiving power.

Your physical body is actually a broadcasting and receiving station specifically designed by creative intelligence for the use of your entity in the environmental conditions to be found on this earth. You may increase its sensitivity only through a development of your own soul, since the body itself responds through the desires and feelings generated in the consciousness.

It is amazing when you consider how little you have had to do with the creation of your own body. It was provided for you, as you know, by a creative act of your father and mother. From the moment of conception, an intelligence within this embryo took charge and supervised and directed the formation of the body you now occupy.

You possessed this body form several years before you were actually conscious of your existence in this life. In the face of this evidence, should you doubt that provision has already been made by this same intelligence for creation and occupancy of a spiritual form when you leave this earth?

Since every kind of intelligence requires *form* in which to manifest itself, you can confidently expect to encounter form throughout all the planes of existence. You were not born into a vacuum on this earth, and when you die, you cannot go into oblivion. There is no such thing in the universe as nothingness, for even nothingness, so-called, is something not yet recognized!

Astronomers now tell us that they have evidence of new, vast universes in the process of creation on the outermost rims of perceivable space—great rings of nebulae, each immensely bigger than our entire Milky Way! Sir James Jeans, the great English scientist, is authority for the statement that "the universe probably contains as many stars as the total number of grains of sand on all the sea shores of the world!" And God is within, behind, and beyond all of this, mindful in an inconceivable way of every pulse beat of every living creature in all the worlds within worlds, high and low, big and small, throughout His ever-expanding, boundless, endless, and surpassingly glorious creation!

To think that we, of human origin, possessing such transcendent possibilities for soul development, should have so perverted these spiritual laws and thus thrown away our priceless opportunities for true advancement in understanding of the Self, of our fellow man, and of the real nature of God in this great universe in which we live.

But God is not impatient. He has given us endless time and space in which to work out our destiny—if not here, then in what we regard as a hereafter, which is only an extension of our consciousness to a new and higher body form in a new environment.

The laws of nature make demands upon you in this life which you must respect if you are to develop and retain good health. This applies on all planes of your being—physical, mental, and spiritual. But nature has not created the fads and fancies of special spiritual diets, abnormal abstinences from sex expression, and peculiar ritualistic observances as a price you must pay for peace of mind and health of body. This has been man's own doing, influenced by ignorance, superstition, and wrong religious interpretation.

A simple, safe rule is "Moderation in all things at all times." The functions of your body and your mind were placed there for your intelligent self-control and use. Otherwise they would not have been given you. This pertains, as well, to the sex organs without which you would not have come into existence nor could you pass on the gifts of life to your children.

Some religions have painted the picture of a sexless life

beyond, with the implication that man is compelled to create himself in shame and sin on this earth but will be de-sexed and spiritualized upon arrival in heaven. This concept is in direct violation of all law and reason since it is everywhere evident, throughout the universe, that the male and female principles of creation are everlastingly at work forming new universes through the attraction and repulsion of positive and negative forces, thus bringing about constant evolutionary and expanding changes and developments in all forms of life.

It is unthinkable, then, that man and woman surrender their sex upon entering the so-called life of the spirit. To do so would be to surrender their very personalities, to give up the very core and center and nature of their creative beings, and to exist as sterile nonentities. More unthinkable than that, it would mean the complete sabotaging and sacrificing of all the fine values built up by individual man and woman through a loving and understanding companionship on earth. To what end? To appease a merciless, wrathful God who created them with sex organs in the first place?

Sex is one of the great mysteries still to be solved, and largely because religion has conceived it to be evil and has not permitted man to discover its spiritual purpose and significance.

In consideration of these facts, our old ideas of heaven must be scrapped to permit acceptance of rational, progressive states of existence in keeping with enlightened reason and faith. With all the authority of the Church in its pronouncements upon the after-life, it has never ventured or been able to locate heaven in time and space. Children and adults alike have inquired, "Just where *is* heaven?" and have received vague, unsatisfying answers. Many, however, have been led to visualize heaven or paradise as existing in some far-off, remote and inaccessible place in the sky which can only be reached under the guidance of angels. They hope, or have faith, that they are going to be transported there in some miraculous fashion at death.

Few of us stop to think that we actually do not know the location of our own planet in the universe, let alone the exact location of heaven. We do know that our ball of earth, together with the other planets, our sun and moon, are traveling through space and *have been* for untold millions of years, and that all other galaxies about us are also in flight. We may well ask: "Where are we? Where have we been? Where are we going?"

We have made as fundamental a mistake in our concept of the nature of heaven as we have in our previous concept that the earth was flat. Because we have not understood the nature of death, we have separated ourselves from eternity when we are living *in* eternity *now!*

Realizing this, heaven is then a *state of being,* and heaven can and should exist, at all times, where we are—and we should live so that we remain in that "heavenly state."

Death only transports us to a new plane of being, and we are separated from this earth more by *dimension* and difference in vibratory rates than by distance. The only real distance is in mind. Two human souls can sit in the same room and be so opposite in views and so filled with antagonism as to be miles apart. Two beings can be so close in thought that, though they exist in different worlds, they are actually *one.*

When the right concept of heaven is given to the peoples of the world, they will be encouraged to strive to bring about "heaven-on-earth," rather than waiting to find heaven after death.

The only hope of poor, downtrodden people, who have lost the urge for self-development and have despaired of ever rising above their sordid life conditions, has been in the promise of "a heavenly existence" in a hereafter. But the laws of the universe are *impersonal* in their operation. Each individual can take over into the next life only the spiritual qualities he has built for himself here. There will be no transformation of character or intelligence or "purifying of souls" in "the twinkling of an eye" at the moment of death or at the "sound of the trumpet."

Our "heavenly state" will only increase here and hereafter as we increase, through spiritual development, our understanding of self and the underlying spiritual principles which rule the progress of all things in God's great universe.

If you have entered the after-life with strongly fixed concepts and preconceived ideas as to what you are going to find there, you can expect to go through a longer or shorter period of adjustment, living in an in-between world created by your own thoughts in opposition to conditions as they actually are. Highly advanced souls who have been able to enter the after-life realm at will, have brought back reports of numbers of human souls existing in a state of indescribable confusion and perplexity because of low spiritual development, inability to recognize clearly what has happened to them, and a steadfast clinging to false concepts, all of which has been keeping them close to their former conditions on earth.

Consider the fact of your entrance into this life on earth. Were you immediately aware of your existence here and did you, at once, adapt yourself to your environment? You know it required quite a few years and the guidance of your elders, who had experienced all this ahead of you, before you could be on your own.

All great developments are slow. God and nature are not in a hurry. You can take as much time as you choose to reach a certain development, but you may penalize yourself in the process by not developing faster. The rewards of spiritual growth are certain and unfailing, even though they may not be immediately apparent on the surface. Nothing that your soul has really gained can ever be taken away from it. But the higher spiritual development and comprehension you have acquired in this life, the better prepared you will be to take up the new activities and interests which are awaiting you in the life beyond.

Again, you must compare what is to come with what has gone before. In your life on earth, no matter how much you might desire it, you cannot jump from kindergarten into high school. This attainment is reached only through effort on your part and the corresponding passage of time it requires. Should you travel to a foreign country which possesses different laws and customs and conditions, however prepared you might be, it would take you a while to adapt yourself to all the elements in this new environment. This same adjustment period will be necessary in the after-life.

Separation from those you love on earth is necessarily a shock since emotional ties are strong enough to reach across barriers of time, space, and even dimension. You have the great advantage, however, of knowing that you have survived death, while those you have left on earth, regardless of how deep their faith, are cruelly torn by your physical loss and have difficulty visualizing you in another existence.

Possessing the assurance that those you love will join you, in time, on your side of life, you can put your mind at rest concerning them. If your soul is sufficiently developed to be ready for active participation in the work and interests open to you, you may well decide that those you have left on earth must continue their experience there as best they can, while you look forward instead of backward, tending to your own further development until the day you will be reunited.

Those whose minds have been prepared for the change called "death" and who have looked forward to this transition as a great adventure, will find thrilling experiences awaiting them. They will possess the spiritual power and awareness to pass through the in-between world and reach higher levels of activity and associations. These souls will busy themselves with their new interests, accepting their new environment, freed of any emotional ties to earth conditions. They will be interested in seeking out friends and close relations who have gone before and enjoying reunion with them. In some instances, the souls they seek will have become so advanced or be engaged in work at such a distance that some time may elapse before they can be found.

If you had relatives in California, a place you had never been, and you suddenly and unexpectedly arrived out there, you would first have to get your bearings and then be guided to their homes, with the chance that they might be away upon your arrival. Those who were free would hasten to greet you at their earliest opportunity, to enjoy a good talk over old times together, then to show you the wonders of California, and if you had come to stay, to help you locate a home of your own and become happily adjusted to your new environment. Under all normal circumstances, the same consideration may be expected in the after-life.

It is my conviction that children and infants who arrive on the other side are cared for in loving homes and schools. Again, this care is patterned after earth institutions, only on a higher level.

Color and race persist, but with the degree of soul quality the distinguishing factor in each individual. There are, without doubt, creatures of human status or higher, of varied colors and races, on countless other worlds, also in process of evolving their souls. Mankind on earth has made the mistake of giving higher evaluation to some colors and races than others. Each was created for some specific purpose and place in God's creation. Each should be interested, then, in striving to achieve his *own perfection* rather than trying to dominate or emulate another.

There are many so ill-prepared for a future state that they desire to cling to the past and strive in every way possible to reach and associate themselves with friends and those they love on earth. Such souls have what might be termed a low quality of energy which keeps them close to the earth plane in a static in-between world condition for so long as they persist in expending that energy downward rather than upward.

No young man or woman on earth can develop needed qualities of self-reliance and character who remains too closely attached to his old home ties. There comes a time when each must step out on his own and make his own decisions and face life for himself. You are in much this position when you find yourself cut off from your earthly home and facing the necessity of adjusting yourself to this after-life environment.

On earth, in the early days of America, when the pioneers entered this new country, they overcame, through their own efforts and experience, the obstacles they had to face and eventually adapted themselves to the conditions and environment encountered. They then welcomed other settlers, giving them the benefit of their acquired wisdom so that they might be made to "feel at home" and soon be equipped to take an active, useful part in the new life around them.

In much the same way, many souls of those who have departed this life some time before are engaged in a service to those now arriving in helping them familiarize themselves with the new surroundings, clearing their confused minds of false and restricting concepts, and removing their fears of eternal punishment and damnation.

Many humans have died with the conviction and belief that they would "know not anything" till Judgment Day. Since all concepts, right or wrong, are realities to each individual for so long as these concepts exist, the false ones must be corrected in order to free that individual's consciousness and truly liberate his soul.

Human beings finding themselves alive after death, when they had expected a cessation of consciousness until the day of resurrection, often cannot immediately believe that death has occurred and feel that they have somehow been caught in some peculiar state of suspended animation and should be able to take up their physical existence again.

But this is a live universe—not a dead one—and the change we call death is simply the means nature has provided for life to pass from a lower to a higher state. It does not stand to reason that once God, the Great Intelligence, has launched us as self-conscious creatures on the ocean of life, we would be snuffed out after a few short developing years on earth, "knowing not anything" until some far-distant day and a trumpet call.

If we do not self-consciously survive death and continue our existence at once, with the demise of the body, we will *remain* dead. But there is every spiritual evidence that life is continuous. We must always have existed in some form, if only in the inconceivable mind of God, the Father-Mother of this universe, or we wouldn't be here today.

The stupendous "blueprint" for the universal scheme of

life included specifications for our own being, however infinitesimal our being may seem to us in relation to the universe as a whole. Whatever has gone before in the indescribable passage of time prior to our arrival at self-conscious existence as human creatures, we have the evidence now that we are a vital part of life. And once having reached this awareness, with the consequent memory of our experience and identity, we need never more lose such awareness. Instead, this awareness will be forever increased as we add to our sensory perceptions through experience and self-development gained in this world and the boundless worlds to come.

God has work for all *qualifying* souls to do. He—and the laws of the universe—are not interested in creating new souls and holding them in unconscious bondage to death for some hundreds, thousands, or even millions of years, to be finally resurrected for a choosing of "the elect" and the eternal damning of "the lost."

Without death, this world could not be a universe of change. Death is the means by which the developing soul of man takes unto itself new forms as it evolves into higher planes of being—forms possessing the necessary elements required on each new plane. Death from this earth will, therefore, not be the only death you will experience. You will lay aside one body after another in the course of your evolution from dimension to dimension, each dimension containing a world of activity and possibilities for development as wonderful, in itself, as this earth has been.

Your time will be taken up with much more practical, worthwhile, and inspiring experiences than eternally playing on harps or singing praises to God, who desires only that you show your love for Him through your deeds and thoughts.

As an earthly parent, wouldn't you tire of sitting on a throne and keeping your children in worshipful servitude, doing nothing throughout an eternity but singing praises to you? You know you would become bored and greatly irritated in an extremely short time and call a halt to all this nonsense, ordering your children to stop wasting time and get out and do something useful!

As far as death is concerned, you are dying in many ways *every day*. Every thought has form and, as you change your concepts, old thought-forms die. The death of many thoughts and ideas you have held in the past has given you new life.

Your physical body itself is the result of thought-forms and design. It was conceived by intelligence—intelligence directs and permeates every cell of it—and when your body dies, this intelligence withdraws from these cells, leaving only a shell behind. But, as I have repeatedly stated, intelligence requires form in which to manifest itself, and so it designs and creates its own forms on all levels of life. You exist in a body on earth and it is unthinkable that your emergence from this body into another existence will not find you clothed in a new form, suited to the new environment.

This form will not be "pure spirit." It will possess substance as seemingly real as the collection of atoms comprising your present body. There will be electrochemical conditions peculiar to this state of existence and laws governing their function, just as consistent as the physical laws with which you are acquainted here.

From intimate sources in communication with advanced souls who I am convinced have experienced contact with the next life, I can give you this picture of it: when you make the change called death you will find that you will require a form of air and water and food of a quality and character adaptable to this body. You will find that nature has surrounded you with a higher form of trees, plants, flowers, and animals which exist within that dimension and in the more refined soil of this after-life. You will discover that the principle of "like attracting like" operates in this life as it has on earth. People of radically different grades of intelligence do not ordinarily gravitate or associate together, here or hereafter.

I have been told by highly evolved individuals and I have sensed that ignorance and wrong thinking and misconduct will still have to be combatted on the lower levels of this life after death, for a constant stream of undeveloped souls is arriving who need reeducation and rehabili-

tation. Just as man on earth has set up institutions of
learning to serve as fountains of knowledge and reposi-
tories of all past acquired wisdom, those in the after-life
have, long since, established great schools for study and
experience. Here the work is with minds more than bodies, with causes rather than effects. In place of punishment, prevention of further misconduct through enlightenment is the aim.

Each soul is given, when ready, an enlarged concept of
God, the Great Intelligence, freed of the sectarian interpretation it may have acquired on earth. This removes, at
once, all previous antagonisms, misunderstandings, and
prejudices, and establishes everyone's spiritual concept
upon a common, harmonious foundation.

Since thoughts can be perceived on this plane of existence, those with evil intent automatically segregate themselves from right-minded souls of constructive purpose.
Yet many highly developed souls elect to work with those
who need guidance and encouragement in order to rise
above the states of mind they have carried over from earth
life.

There are some souls so steeped in the developed evil
natures of their possessors that all offers of help and enlightenment are rejected. These souls have identified themselves with the destructive principles of nature and may be
eventually disintegrated and destroyed, if their entities
willfully continue to pursue the same devolutionary path
of life.

Evolution employs both constructive and destructive
principles in its functioning. The destructive principles
perform a constructive purpose when they eventually destroy that which has completely lost or surrendered its
usefulness. Thus it is not the decree of God that certain of
His human creatures should be consigned to hell, but it is
they, themselves, who ultimately pass judgment upon their
own conduct. They do this by long-continued refusal to attune themselves to the God-power within them. They sink
so low as to lose all contact with it and, as a consequence,
lose also their own self-conscious "I am I" identity.

To realize what this would mean, it is imperative that

you understand the relationship of this "I am I" consciousness to you. Have you considered that the inner voice which gives you the constant consciousness of your own identity is also saying, "I am I," in the mind of every other human? Your name is not the real you because it can be changed while your identity remains the same. Therefore, it should be clear to you that every human being who has ever lived, and who is alive now, and who will be born and live in the future, has possessed, does possess, and will possess this same ever-present consciousness of "I am I," the equal presence of God in all his self-conscious creatures.

This "I am I" awareness of identity, then, comes to all creatures, in all worlds, at the instant they reach a state of evolution capable of making self-conscious attunement with the universal God-power. Once this attunement has been reached through evolutionary process, all offspring thereafter are born with body instruments capable of maintaining this attunement. But once the "I am I" identity has entered the consciousness of the evolving creature, conferring upon it the power of free will and free choice, it is then held to individual accountability for its own spiritual progress.

For so long as this progress is continued on the upward spiral in this life and the next, the individual soul enjoys an ever-expanding awareness of its own "I am I" identity in God. But if the thoughts and acts of an individual become increasingly low and degrading, he reverts to the time in his early animal ancestry when no "I am I" consciousness existed, and then, with his hold released upon this part of God which has dwelled in him, all awareness of self is lost forever.

This is the penalty nature imposes for not making constructive use of the physical, mental, and spiritual opportunites she offers on every level of life. Thus it is well to remember that life is a free gift from God, your Creator, but with and through it you have to *earn* immortality.

11. A WAY OF SPIRIT COMMUNICATION

WHEN YOU DIE and enter a higher dimension, you are removed from the plane of life in which those on earth still exist. You have not lost the dimensional capacities you had before but have taken on some new ones, thus extending not only your conscious awareness but your capacity for expression in new and expanded directions.

Is it so illogical then to consider that those you loved on earth, not sharing your elevated state and possession of new powers, should be unable to reach you with their ordinary sensory faculties and therefore would have no way of proving your continued existence unless they, themselves, developed a conscious knowledge of how to utilize their higher powers of mind—powers which are equipped to function on spirit levels and thus overcome the natural physical barriers existing between the two planes. You, however, from your elevated position, would have the capacity for communication if channels could be opened up in the minds of those you have left behind.

Intelligence is the only communicating medium between one entity and another. Bodies themselves have no intelligence and obviously no power of communication. For one on earth to make actual contact with your discarnate intelligence, it would be necessary to bring into play the spiritual perceptions existing within each soul, and few human beings have yet recognized and developed these perceptions.

In other words, soul must communicate with soul, for each then exists in the same medium.

But the conscious mind and physical sensory apparatus of man were not designed for, and are totally incapable of, making contact with any higher intelligence. There have been many instances, however, when the conscious mind of man has been temporarily quieted through sleep, that contact has been made between the soul of a departed one and our own inner consciousness, resulting in a vivid dream impression, occasionally so real as to give a carry-over feeling that we have been in touch with the other world.

It has been possible, also, through developed methods of meditation and receptivity consciously to activate these higher sensory powers contained in the subconscious. Under these induced conditions, one may receive vivid mental pictures, inspirational flashes, and seeming messages or feelings which can be interpreted as coming, if not from the beyond, from an intelligence possessing far greater knowledge than our present awareness.

I have received thousands of letters from earnest men and women who have been seeking the truth, insofar as it could be learned, concerning the great question of life after death and whether or not it might be possible to communicate with those who have departed. They have asked me what I thought of spirit mediums, trumpet seances, materialization, direct voice, automatic writing, and if they themselves should sit for development in "psychic circles."

I have had to tell these people frankly that, while I am convinced many people possess varying degrees of psychic power and can on occasion demonstrate telepathy, clairvoyance, precognition and like phenomena, I can not recommend any such thing, and I must particularly warn them against opening up their own minds to unknown psychic influences.

As I have previously stated, the whole field of psychic

phenomena and so-called spirit communication lends itself so ideally to trickery and deception of every sort that shameful fraud can be practiced upon otherwise intelligent and discerning men and women who, deeply moved by grief and sentiment, are willing to believe most anything without question.

The spirit communication and fortune-telling racket is a hundred-million-dollar-a-year business. For every so-called psychic who is genuine there are literally a hundred fakes. This percentage against you is too great for you to risk your money, your time, and your emotions upon. If you do get in a "psychic development circle" where some phenomena are in evidence, unless you exercise extreme caution, you may attune yourself to some influences of a low order which will cause you emotional and mental distress and which can be thrown off only with great difficulty.

You must realize that the after-life contains every type of human soul from the lowest to the highest, just as we have on earth. When you open the higher centers of your mind to make contact with intelligences without and have not developed the proper self-conscious, directional, protective control, it is just as though you were living on a busy thoroughfare and opened the door of your house to whatever types of humans might be passing, including the worst possible riffraff. But, because these intelligences are now invisible to you, and beyond detection and examination by your five physical senses, unless you are a trained "sensitive" you have no developed power of discrimination and may permit the wrong influences to enter and take possession of your consciousness.

For this reason, those who dabble innocently in the field of the psychic should beware. They do not know with what tremendous forces of good and evil they are playing. Nor should these inexperienced investigators permit themselves to be hypnotized or attempt to develop trance states or take on any condition which would open up the possibility of making their ego subservient to any other intelligence, either within or without the body.

Each human soul is protected and insulated against the direct trespass upon, or imposition of, the will of any other soul, unless this protection and insulation is surrendered by that soul, either of its own volition or through the subtle influence and suggestion of a designing mind in which trust has been placed.

It is imperative that you retain, at all times, your own free-will control of your ego in all of its manifestations, dealings, and associations with others. Only in this way can you be certain of maintaining your absolute integrity and your contact with unperverted and undistorted truth which exists within your own soul through its relationship to God, the Great Intelligence.

Startling things can be demonstrated through hypnotism. The intelligence of the indwelling entity can be put aside and the body caused to react to suggestions of heat and cold, humor and ridicule, shame and praise, fear and courage, pain and joy, and all other human emotions, much after the fashion of a mechanical robot. Hypnotism —the control of your mind and body by another human being on this plane of life—is not too much different from the type of control exercised by the will of a designing, discarnate personality. In either case, once you have surrendered yourself to the will of another intelligence you will, thereafter, have great difficulty calling your soul your own.

Advertising is a form of mass hypnotism through suggestion. You want something someone else has because it has been made appealing to you through an attractive picture and copy in a magazine or newspaper, and you are given the urge to buy it. Propaganda, cleverly worded to arouse your emotions and to cause you to think along certain lines, is aimed at you by political factions. Friends and relatives who desire you to comply with their wishes will try artful means of persuasion upon you. Your mind is already subject to many influences, good or bad, depending upon their source and motivation, but the most subtle influences of all, and those which can do the most damage are those that are psychic, which strike at your mind and soul, often reaching you through your emotions and sentiments.

Try to conceive, if you can, the boundless ocean of intelligence in which you exist. Each thought of every human being has a rate and character of vibration and is being transmitted unconsciously into space. The mental ether about you is thus filled with vibratory thought of mankind, high and low. Add to this the vibratory thought of discarnate intelligence existing in the in-between world, close to earth, and you have some small idea of the colossal activity of ever-changing and intermingling thought forms, many of which are charged with such destructive emotions as greed, hate, prejudice, and lust.

Have you seen a great city, such as Chicago, in the grip of a smoke-fog which blots out the upper stories of skyscrapers and so blankets the town as to turn day into night? Wrong thinking can and does produce what might be termed low-lying clouds of thought forms which you must break through in order to reach the higher, finer thought forms of developed souls who reside on the plane called heaven, beyond this borderland or in-between world of confused and disturbed entities.

This is one of the basic reasons why true spirit communication has been so difficult and fraught with a certain amount of mental and physical peril to the uninitiated. You have evidence of many unprincipled charlatans and impostors on earth. Unhappily, there are just as many in the in-between world of the afterlife and there always will be until mankind reaches a higher degree of spiritual development on earth.

I have emphasized the fact that a part of God dwells within you, that you possess a soul which has the potentialities of immortality and which only you can ultimately destroy by your own wrong deeds and thoughts. I repeat that you are, or can be, as close to God on your level of consciousness, as any other human being, either here or hereafter.

There is a great mystery contained in the fact that your personality is exclusively different from that of any other human being but that your "I am I" consciousness of identity is *exactly the same*. Because it is the same, you are really *one* in consciousness with all other human beings and with all self-conscious creatures who have ever lived, or who will live on all inhabited worlds throughout time and space in God's great universe. You must realize that while this inner voice is saying, "I am I" to you, it is saying "I am I" to every living self-conscious being in the cosmos!

Closely related as you are, through possessing an exactly similar awareness of identity in God, the Great Intelligence, you should be able to realize the full import of the admonition, "Do unto others as you would that they should do unto you," for you are actually injuring your own self when you injure any other self, each a vital part of universal consciousness in individual form.

To reach and communicate with those who have gone on requires enlargement of your own concepts and a realization that your soul is not limited by the dimensions of time and space.

In my telepathic experiments with Sir Hubert Wilkins, when he was over three thousand miles away in the far north and I was in my apartment in New York City, I was able to sense that he had a severe toothache on the *one* day in five months that a tooth had troubled him, causing him to fly to Edmonton to get it filled! I felt, for the moment, that *I* was Wilkins and it was *my* tooth which had ached. In that flashing instant when the impression came, *I* was not conscious of any distance between us.

If you can once get the comprehension of what it means to be saying, "I am I" in unison with all human beings everywhere, then direct your inner self to make contact with a specific identity in this stream of "I am I" consciousness, there will come to you the sudden *feeling* that you are *one* with that entity. There can be no break or gap in the ocean of intelligence permeated by "I AM!"

When, through meditation, you reach up into the next dimension seeking communion with a departed one, contact is established in much the same way. Do not expect, ordinarily, to receive any message in words. You may get your most convincing and satisfying response in the form of a deep, unmistakable feeling of nearness and understanding.

When you feel as another human being feels, you are in an attunement with that person much closer than words.

This is the highest aim of love and what is meant when it is said that "two can think and act as one."

There can be no communion on any plane without *feeling*. The deeper the feeling, the closer the communion, and the closer the communion, the greater the understanding of each other.

Feeling is an explainable attribute of consciousness. Feeling is behind our five physical senses. Feeling is the *interpreter* of every impression that comes to us from within or without.

You see, and you have feelings about what you see.

You hear, and you feel moved or unmoved by what you hear.

You taste, and you feel pleased or displeased by what you taste.

You touch, and you feel attracted or repulsed by what you touch.

You smell, and you feel drawn to or driven away by the odor.

Feeling is the great universal language. When we have learned to rely more upon *feeling,* we will have greatly extended our awareness.

At present we have only developed the power to communicate understandably with our kind of intelligence. We cannot talk intelligibly to a tree, a flower, or a dog. Our only medium of communication or possible affinity with a tree, a flower, or a dog is through *feeling.* As yet we cannot sense the type of consciousness possessed by this tree, this flower, and this dog. But there will come a day in our development when we will converse with them as freely as with our fellow men.

Not only that, but because time and space constitute no barrier in the "I am I" consciousness, we will fix our minds on self-conscious intelligences on other inhabited worlds and communicate with them by means of a *sensitized feeling faculty,* despite all differences in language!

There are different grades of intelligence in all things and the nature of all things is determined by the grade of intelligence forming or shaping those things.

Consciousness is *intelligence in action*—and all consciousness has *feeling*.

There is an electrical, magnetic quality about feeling. It holds particles of matter together. If the feeling changes, the magnetism is broken and the particles break up, seeking new affinities on the basis of like attracting like. You *feel* that a certain thing is going to happen which means that you have pictured the possibility in your mind and this feeling is even now magnetically drawing the elements and conditions and circumstances to you in response to this pictured desire.

You *feel* in a moment of deep, heartfelt spiritual meditation that you wish to reach someone you love in the after-life, and this feeling, if properly dispatched, makes contact with that soul. You may not get a response at once, but if you will curb your doubts and anxiety and quiet your conscious mind and emotions, there will come to you in time a satisfying experience.

This awareness is developed while remaining in a self-conscious state, without resorting to trances or psychic circles or mediums or any other mechanisms or forces outside yourself.

How much more logical that the one you love should seek you out if you open the door to him in the privacy of your own home and heart, rather than by trying to find him through some stranger at so much a "sitting."

Much truth will one day be revealed through means of scientifically developed and controlled psychic powers. The door of a great, new, wonderful world is slowly being pushed ajar to expose the true nature of spiritual powers, which have always existed but which mankind, with its almost totally mistaken reliance upon the testimony of the five physical senses, has been too blind to sense.

It is impossible to give you a specific technique of spiritual communication. This is beyond words, but you will discover this technique for yourself if you read between the lines of what has been written and give conscientious thought to your own spiritual development. The clues for communication are all contained in this chapter, together with the very sober warnings of pitfalls to be encountered or avoided.

If you have the perseverance, the courage, and the faith in yourself and the God-power within, to penetrate the wilderness as it exists at present, you may emerge into the spiritually illumined plane which has been reached by others before you and enjoy, with them, the certain knowledge that, in the soul sense, there is *no* basic separation from those who love.

12. HOW TO PREPARE FOR A FUTURE LIFE

THE SUREST WAY to find yourself prepared for a future life when it comes is to live each day as though it were to be your last.

Few people, if they knew for a certainty that they were to die within the next twenty-four hours, could or would be indifferent to this fact. There is something sobering and compelling about the approach of death which demands that an individual take stock of himself, whether or not he is of religious turn of mind.

Of course, if you have waited until the last day of your life to give thought and attention to your state of preparedness for such a transition, you may well find yourself like a passenger carried away on a train to a strange destination without the proper baggage.

Stop now, and ask yourself what essential values you have developed in life thus far. What do you possess in yourself that cannot be taken away, no matter what happens, and which can be of continuous service to you now as well as hereafter?

If you should be stripped of all earthly possessions and physically removed from friends and those you love, taken to a new environment entirely, and equipped with a new body form, recognizably similar to your one on earth but free of any deformity, what would you yourself bring with you with which to face this great experience?

It would have to be developed qualities of soul, contained within your consciousness, together with a memory of all past experiences and the abilities which that past experience had given you. If your life had been filled with hate and greed and lust and prejudice, your soul would be burdened and hampered with these thoughts and feelings and, since like attracts like, you would find yourself gravitating to levels of intelligence possessing low soul development similar to your own.

Whereas, on earth, money has been power, in the impersonal economy of nature, knowledge of self is power. What you don't know about yourself can definitely hurt you and retard your spiritual growth.

Your judgment of others in this life may have been based upon their social standing rather than their character. In fact, today, there is widespread disregard for character-building as a purported asset in life. It is not often the spiritually endowed person who wins the race for material gain. He is usually left in the dust by many inferior to him in development who have ruthlessly trampled him underfoot by their employment of dishonest, unfair, and even strong-armed tactics to get there first.

George Bernard Shaw is reported to have said, upon learning of Gandhi's assassination: "This just goes to show—it doesn't pay to be too good!"

We are only one broad jump, as human beings, beyond the day of primitive man. He robbed and slew with a club to gain his ends on earth but we, with our greater intelligence, have vastly improved on his methods. We now threaten whole nations of people with atomic bombs, military power, or economic pressure if they oppose us. We blacklist and smear or annihilate any individual or group of individuals who disagree too strongly with us, even though they may speak the truth. Church and state are now lining up for a battle to the death throughout the world. Unless a great and miraculous change comes about in the mass consciousness of mankind in the next few years, man's long fight up through the darkness of his own ignorance may end in another long night.

Those who seek to dominate must destroy or subjugate intelligence. They must destroy man's freedom of thought and freedom of speech. They have not recognized the great basic truth and principle that, "To be free, you must *first* let others be free." Thus, they would take whole nations of people into bondage along with themselves.

Since you are alive today in a world so abounding in great possibilities for the physical, mental, and spiritual advancement of man, you must also be mindful that there was never a time in our recorded history when this future of man has been so threatened. There are tremendous forces at work in the world, motivated by hate, which, unless checked and their destructive feelings eliminated through new understanding, will most certainly precipitate a third World War.

Whether or not you, as an individual, wish to remain isolated from what is happening on this planet, new methods of communication and the interdependent economic relationships which exist today will suck you into this situation sooner or later, and compel you to do something about it in self-defense.

Consider for a moment the mental and emotional venom which is daily pouring into the stream of consciousness which runs through all mankind. It is as though the sewage of wrong thinking were being dumped in a great reservoir serving all humans and this pollution of the water were reaching each individual as he taps it by turning on the faucet of his own mind. You cannot escape the taint of such wrong thinking even though you may be far removed from its source.

What is happening in Europe, in China, in the Middle East, in Russia, and elsewhere is having its repercussions here and throughout the world. Evil thoughts and evil conditions spread like a plague. Man is abusing the great creative laws of the universe, creating for himself, through wrong thinking, all manner of wrong results which are leading, unless corrected, to his own destruction.

Not realizing the great power of thought, we have been striving to eliminate the effects brought about by thought rather than getting at the cause which is thought itself. Once thought has given form to ideas, these forms will continue to exist until their originating thought has been changed. Then the old forms must die for lack of nourishment and support.

It is impossible to oppose thought with armed might. Victories can be won on the battlefield and lost in the peace conference, with thought remaining unchanged. Ignorance and prejudice are only removed and replaced by knowledge. Money cannot, in itself, buy a change of heart or a change of mind.

Another war will most certainly come, in due time, unless people everywhere gain a new understanding of their relationship to each other, their actual kinship in consciousness, their realization that each is responsible for the other, and an increased appreciation of the value of human life.

You and all human beings are therefore presented with a great challenge which transcends in importance your individual interests and desires. The problem with which world leaders are actually confronted, if they but knew it, is how to reach mass consciousness, cutting through iron curtains of prejudice, hatred, and ignorance, and giving it new concepts so powerful, appealing, and inspiring as to change the thinking of these peoples through eliminating the terrific tensions which exist in certain world sectors and which are nearing a breaking point that will eventually engulf all humanity.

It has been difficult for man to visualize himself as being a part of any other consciousness or thing beyond the *boundary* of his own physical body. He has likewise limited himself in concept to the *boundary* of the country in which he lives. His thinking in strong nationalistic terms has caused him to resist co-operation, beyond a certain point, with citizens and governments of other countries. He has fought to protect his boundaries from encroachment and violation as he also fights to defend a trespass upon or abuse of his own person.

Eventually, a United States of the World *must* come in which the freedom-loving rights of all men are protected and all concepts of boundaries separating different colors and races from each other are removed. It will then be possible, with the present race and color tensions relieved, for each race and color to devote its energies toward self-development and to grow in harmony through the realization that we are all equal in the sight of our God, whatever our individual faith, and that we are here to serve one another to the end that the heaven of peace and happiness we seek may exist here as well as hereafter.

The feelings of fear, suspicion, distrust, and the clash of conflicting ideologies can bring only chaos in time. Your future life on earth, as well as in the life beyond, will be affected by what is materializing in the world today as a result of this great turbulence in thought. The mental forces at work are so potent that they are beyond the reach and influence of any church or government or factional appeals, however sincerely presented.

A new intelligent force is needed in the world—*the force of the human spirit*—untouched by the influence of special interest, prejudicial attitudes, specific hates, religious intolerance, economic aggression, political ambition, and unyielding ignorance or desire for domination. Could this human spirit be so liberated in the minds and hearts of men, it could free the world in an incredibly short time by changing the motivation of mankind, making its regenerating influence felt in high places and low. The soul of man, unadulterated and given an opportunity to express itself, possesses an unerring sense of truth and justice.

It is only when man attempts to divide up the truth, and segregate and distort it through organization, that he loses the very thing he seeks. The truth cannot be bounded by the walls of a church, the confines of a college campus, the laboratories of a scientist, the laws of a land, or the covers of a book. It is as free as the principle behind it and, if trampled to earth, will rise again in the spirit of truth-seeking men.

It is unthinkable that the rank and file of human beings on earth today desire another world war. And yet their thoughts are being turned in this direction by every means at the disposal of certain world leaders and factions. We must all assume a share of the guilt in this horrifying trend toward self-destruction. We have continually sought to cure the ills of the world, as must be emphasized again, by treating effects instead of causes. We have tried to cover up the sores of the last world war but we have not healed them. These same sores are infecting the world anew.

There is no inference intended that many leaders in church, state, business, and all walks of life are not fine-charactered men and women, but their serviceability to the world as a whole is limited for the most part by the very positions they occupy and the fixedness of their thought concerning these positions. This is a natural human concomitant of all past experience and development, but we have arrived at a crossroads in human evolution on this planet which requires a clearing away of old concepts, old ways of doing things, and old rock-ribbed alliances and zones of influence, either for or against nations, which give birth to new enmities and new wars.

But if it were possible for all world leaders and the world powers they represent to put aside this interest in *self* for a genuine interest in the *whole* of humanity, then each self would be immeasurably benefited thereby. Such thinking and such points of view must come into the consciousness of man before he can lift himself from the mire of his own creating.

The inability of man to adjust his differences in ideology and to establish a common basis of understanding and co-operation, freed of fear of aggression and suppression of individual human rights, will eliminate all possibility of universal brotherhood in our time and, perhaps, for a long, long time to come.

Regardless of conditions, whether good or bad, you must have the courage to live and raise your children with the right concepts of life so that the next generation will be able to reach higher states of self-development and spiritual knowledge. Your greatest protection, at all times, is your concentration upon the things and experiences in life which can develop in you lasting values, the kind of mental and spiritual qualities which bring inner happiness and satisfaction. So equipped, you can face whatever is to come with faith and fortitude, knowing that even death will find you not wanting in the soul properties which can make your entrance upon a new life a truly great adventure.

Each mind, freed of false concepts and destructive feelings, withdraws just so much destructive thought from the ocean of consciousness and helps raise its level, thus improving conditions on earth. There will, one day, be found a close relationship between climatic, atmospheric, and geologic conditions and the human mind. Science, through Dr. Rhine's research at Duke University, has already proved the influence of mind over matter. Think what influence the destructive force of mass mind can and does have upon its surroundings in nature! Is it too inconceivable to speculate that even earthquakes may be caused, in part, by emotional unbalance and the volcanic upheaval in world consciousness?

Great faults and cracks in the earth's surface exist from former times in the world's long history. There are theories that sun spots, the gravitational pull of the moon, and other planets also have a bearing on weather, earthquakes, and even upon the time of great eruptions. But man himself may add his destructive vibrations to the sum total and help "pull the trigger" on the natural calamities which are visited upon him.

At any rate, we know beyond any doubt, the harmful influence of wrong thinking upon man himself: how wrong thoughts set up wrong chemical reactions in the body, creating actual poisons in the system; how ill will can make its possessor sick and affect the physical and mental health of those near him; and how wrong mental attitudes of world leaders can so influence a people as to produce world wars.

It isn't the development of atomic power which man fears. It is the use to which man may decide to put atomic power which frightens and appalls him.

Keep in touch by newspaper and radio with what is taking place in the world today. Try to read and listen between the lines of what is being written and said. Let your own inner sense of truth and justice determine for you what is true or false in what you see in print and hear via the mass communication media or in your daily rounds of life. Do not permit yourself to be drawn into any hate or prejudice groups under any guise whatsoever. Hold your mind as free as possible of all destructive thoughts. Be ready to defend your country, if need be, against any actual threats of aggression, but hold a love for all humanity and remember that all men are actually your brothers in consciousness.

There is every evidence that you are an individualized, segmentized part of the "Great I Am," given physical form on this plane of life with opportunity, as a creature of free will and free choice, to evolve your own soul through self-development as you meet the varied experiences here and in the existence to come. Progression is endless, here and hereafter. Once established on the evolutionary upward path, you will gain a greater and greater awareness as time goes on of your identity and the part you are to play in God's great, unfolding scheme of things!

But keep in mind that you are just as much in eternity now as you will be after death. You can be as close to God now as you will be then. Your soul is your link with the infinite. You have been placed on this earth for a definite purpose and you can serve God as much here as you can hereafter. In so doing, you will find yourself best prepared for the after-life.

13. HOW TO FACE DEATH

In Time To Come, when death has been scientifically proved to be the gateway to another life, all fear of death will be removed from the consciousness of mankind.

If this fact were announced today, it would require some centuries before people of all races and creeds would be able, even with this realization, to outgrow the fear of death which has been a part of their animal heritage. As I have stated before, the body cannot testify to any life without itself. Such testimony can only come from the soul of man, which is already linked to the world beyond, as it stores up the experience man gains in this life for use in the next.

Consider once more how limited and confining an eternal life would be if you were required to live it in this one body and on this one planet, however physically perfect your body might have been made. Consider the wonders of the universes upon universes about you and your inability ever actually to visit them or share in the experiences which other worlds hold because of your enforced eternal residence here.

No human mind can comprehend eternity except in terms of the "forever-now." But you can easily conceive that an endless life on this earth would eventually exhaust its interest to the point of monotony. You would have reached the saturation point in variety of experiences and in what you could know about the earth and would long for release from your prison house of flesh.

There is something within your higher consciousness which urges you on toward greater experience and perfection. This something demands change—new scenes, new associations, new opportunities, new knowledge, new inspiration. It is the God-force in man, this vague or vivid awareness as the case may be, that each new day holds the promise of better and finer things. Should this urge continue to exist without the possibility of fulfillment in each tomorrow, you would indeed be in hell.

Brilliant men and women, possessing great knowledge of certain subjects and an enormous desire to advance in their chosen fields, when suddenly denied opportunity for continuation of their work for economic reasons, ill health, or other restrictive circumstances, have lost all interest in life and living, and have even gone so far as to commit suicide.

There must be purpose in life and progress. Without it, nothing has meaning and very little interest. Individuals who have planned to retire at certain ages, anticipating the joys of "doing nothing," have found that this was harder work than activity, and unless they have developed new and worthwhile interests, have often declined in health and spirit, releasing their hold on life.

The spiritually developed person looks forward to his later years, when the harder battles of life have been won and his soul has been enriched by a maturity of experience. He anticipates the increased opportunity he will have for rendering counsel and service to others and for preparing himself, through meditation and study, for the life to come.

God, the Great Intelligence, has wisely provided, through death, a means by which man may increasingly participate in His boundless evolution. This requires that man must pass through a succession of ever higher forms as the nature of his own soul is raised through closer and closer identification with the God-force within. The soul then utilizes each new form it occupies in turn, as the instrument through which it manifests itself, even as it has used the physical form on earth. You may thus expect to die many times in the body and rise again in new forms permitting, each time, greater expression of your own soul and the greater extension of your powers of awareness of the universe about you.

So—why fear death?

It has been my privilege to know a few people who had reached that state of consciousness wherein they had no fear. They *knew* that life did not end at the grave. They *knew* that a wonderful new world awaited them. They *knew* that they would be going to rejoin friends who were actively and happily engaged in work beyond. Their *knowing* was a conviction that faith alone could not bring; it was a conviction born of *inner spiritual experience.*

Feeling that their mission on earth had been served, they eagerly looked forward to release from the body. They told me not to grieve when I should learn of their passing, but to rejoice with them that they had now entered this new and higher state of being. In some instances, these highly developed souls actually knew where they were going and the exact nature of the work they were to be engaged in. They discussed this contemplated future activity with me as naturally as though they were planning to take up residence in a new and different part of this country. They saw beyond the flesh walls of their own body, aware that their *real* existence was not *in* this body and thus could project their thinking, without any break in continuity, beyond the life and existence of their physical form.

This spiritual awareness must come, in time, to all humanity. But until it comes, most humans will still suffer great fears of death.

When the moment of death draws near, however, these fears, in most instances, quite amazingly disappear. A strange, relaxed quiet and calmness comes to the personality from within. The instant that the intelligence in the body knows that recovery is impossible, this fact is communicated to the soul, which prepares to take over and starts the processes which will eventuate in releasing that soul, in its spirit form, from its fleshy instrument.

On occasion, dependent upon the self-conscious receptivity of the personality, the soul may reveal through a vision, or a higher sensory manifestation, a fleeting glimpse of the world beyond, or even of friends whom that identity is soon to join. At other times, the dying individual will have produced for himself, in consciousness, his own earth concepts of heaven and heavenly music, angels, and Christ. He will feel himself to be in the presence of the Master and will die in this faith. Still others, almost separated from the body, will describe themselves as hovering above it and looking down at it. This latter experience is quite common and gives further evidence that intelligence, at death, does leave the body and does not die with it.

Of course, when one is conscious of body pains and various forms of physical distress, as death approaches, it is difficult to retain spiritual composure even with faith and conviction as to one's future. Those, however, who have had the experience of leaving the physical body and returning at will, all testify that it holds no terrors but is quite the most wonderful sensation that can be realized by a human creature.

They point out that we actually die, so to speak, each night when we go to sleep. That sleep, in fact, is the little sister of death. They remind us how much we usually look forward to gaining a good night's rest through sleep and awakening in the morning refreshed, ready for a new start in life. "Death," they say, "is only an awakening from a sleep of the body in a new world just as real as this one has been, and in a new body every bit as substantial as the one we have discarded on earth."

It is easier to face death when one feels he has lived out his allotted time, has accomplished his purpose in life, and is ready for the change. It is much more difficult to be compelled to consider leaving when much remains to be done, when many responsibilities are being left behind, when those close to you are in desperate need of you, and when it seems that fate is being most cruel and unjust in taking you away. You must realize, again, that as free-will creatures on this earth we are subject to accident and misfortune through the operation of physical forces external to us which may cut short our lives before our time. When this happens, an adjustment must be made by those left on earth and by those who go on. They must seek in and through this necessary adjustment, regardless of the hardships imposed, the experiences which will add greatest value to their souls and help compensate those on both sides of life for the temporary loss of physical companionship.

The experiences of no two people on earth have ever been or ever will be the same. *Life is an individual proposition.* We each possess an individual destiny which we help to create by the manner in which we react to the experiences which come to us. But each objective gained only reveals greater and finer objectives to be achieved beyond, and this is the way it will be throughout all eternity.

When those you love who have lived full lives and who wish to go on are seriously ill, do not try to hold them here against their wills. Sons and daughters quite often plead with fathers and mothers to exert their will to live when they are existing in physical forms which have long outlasted their usefulness. There have been many cases wherein elderly parents have actually resisted death and have risen from what could have been their deathbeds at the petition of their children who have emotionally declared a desperate need for them.

I have personal knowledge of one case where a spiritually developed mother of eighty recovered from pneumonia and remained on this earth through sheer force of will alone, at the petition of her middle-aged daughter. Upon being taken ill again, four years later, she called this daughter to her bedside and said: "Anna, I feel it is my time and I want to go. I know that friends dear to me are waiting for me. Won't you tell me that you are willing to let me go?"

"All right, Mother," Anna replied. "If it's your wish, I won't try to hold you here any longer."

An expression of profound relief and peaceful resignation came over the mother's face.

In less than an hour, she died.

If you have lost a child through death, make every effort to control your grief. Each child necessarily has a strong emotional attachment for its parents and especially its mother. As I have pointed out, *deep feeling* knows no boundaries of time or space. You may rest assured that your child is being lovingly cared for—more so in most instances than had it been left an orphan on earth.

It is criminal that fake spirit mediums should pretend to bring back the spirits of children who have passed on some years before, representing them as having the same age and form and intelligence as they had on earth. It is natural for a mother and father to hold to the concept of their child as it existed at the time of death. But freed from their emotional fixations, had they given their reason an opportunity to function, they would clearly perceive that, if life persists beyond the grave, there is progress there as here. This being true, their child would continue its bodily, mental, and spiritual development where it had left off, under the guidance and care of those in the afterlife equipped for such service.

It is, therefore, a great mistake for mothers and fathers not to release their departed child from their fixed concepts, since holding these highly emotional thoughts may have repercussions, at times, upon the consciousness of the child itself. Unthinking fathers and mothers actually expect to greet their infants and young people in heaven, even years after their demise, looking and acting exactly as they did before they passed on. They will see such sons and daughters, in due time, and will recognize them through unmistakable personality features, but their children, if enough time has elapsed, will have changed greatly in form and mind.

Those who are face to face with death often resort to prayer as a means of preparing them to meet their God. In the light of what has herein been said about the nature of God, you may wonder what function prayer now can have in the great scheme of things.

The value of prayer is in no wise lost through this enlarged conception of God and the Universe. Prayer is the soul's recognition of a power far greater than itself and the expression of that soul's profound desire to come in closer attunement with that power and thus to receive the spiritual benefits of such attunement.

A selfish or undeserved request in prayer is rejected by the soul and does not reach the God-consciousness within. A prayer, in order to be "heard" and "answered" by God, the Great Intelligence, must be in line with the individual's actual physical, mental, and spiritual needs. God is not self-consciously aware of the individual prayer but, if the spirit behind it is in accordance with spiritual law, that prayer is eventually answered.

Prayer, then, through crystallizing the power of your own desires for help and service, can unite your soul with the spiritual forces needed to bring that for which you have prayed to pass.

Prayer, asking forgiveness for misdeeds, serves the purpose, if the petitioner is sincere, of cleansing his spirit and giving him new strength of soul.

In time of death, prayer fixes the attention of your mind and soul upon the God-power within and enables you to feel the presence of this power in a deeply satisfying personal sense. Remember, the more you come to know God, thus gaining a greater understanding of your own real self —this "I am I" consciousness—the more personal a Being will God become to you.

Use prayer, then, but use it *intelligently,* not as a *form* or *ritual.* Mechanical repetition of certain words or phrases will not impress God. It is the earnest call of your own self for help and guidance which brings a response from the Father of all things.

Prepare for death by preparing for a new life. Keep your earthly house in order. By that I mean your personal affairs. Maintain them in as orderly shape as possible, at all times. Then, freed of material worries or "things left undone," you can meet this great moment in your life with a clear conscience and consciousness, say what you might wish to say to those you love, and take your departure with resignation and expectation.

Within your soul is contained the knowledge of all that you have been in the timeless past and the potentiality of all that you *can* be in the timeless future. Some day the record of the past will be opened to you and you will see and comprehend the now untold experiences you have passed through on your journey up to the level of God-consciousness. You will understand, too, how arrival at the level of God-consciousness has brought you awareness of your identity and the limitless possibilities of your evolving soul.

ESP RESEARCH ASSOCIATES FOUNDATION

SUITE 1660
UNION NATIONAL PLAZA BLDG.
LITTLE ROCK, ARKANSAS 72201

TO YOU WHO HAVE READ THIS BOOK:

You may have had evidence, through personal experience, of communications you feel you have received from friends and loved ones who have made the transition into the Next Life.

These contacts may have come through one or more types of psychic phenomena such as a mental impression, the feeling of a presence, an apparition, an inner voice, a vivid dream, an out-of-body projection, a trumpet or materializing seance, a telepathic exchange, automatic writing or ouija board messages, etc.

Whatever the form of contact, since the ESP Foundation is making an extensive study of all areas related to cases suggestive of "survival after death," I would appreciate your writing me in detail about what may have happened or be happening to you.

If, in such report as you might care to send us, you would rather your name not be used, this request will be respected.

My thanks for your help in this expanding, invaluable research which can mean so inexpressibly much to every individual life on this planet.

Sincerely,
Harold Sherman
Founder and President